The Ration Book
DIET

Mike Brown
Carol Harris
C.J. Jackson

Photography by Michelle Garrett

SUTTON PUBLISHING

First published in the United Kingdom in 2004 by
Sutton Publishing Limited · Phoenix Mill
Thrupp · Stroud · Gloucestershire · GL5 2BU

British Library Cataloguing in Publication Data
A catalogue record for this book is available from the British Library.

ISBN 0-7509-3944-3

Design: Annie Falconer-Gronow
Colour photography: Michelle Garrett
Nutritionist: Fiona Hunter
Recipe testing: Rebecca Ford

Typesetting and origination by
Sutton Publishing Limited.
Printed and bound in England by
J.H. Haynes & Co. Ltd, Sparkford.

Contents

Introduction

When VE-Day finally came in May 1945, Britain was a very different place from the country it had been in 1939. Six years of war had taken their toll on the fabric of the nation. In many cases the effects were far-reaching in terms of Britain's social, economic and demographic characteristics. But if there was one good thing to have come out of the war then it was food rationing: the war left us healthier as a nation than we had ever been before or have been since.

In this book we have adapted some of the most popular wartime recipes, which, as we have discovered through some very enjoyable tasting sessions, are delicious. We have re-created others to make them more appealing to the twenty-first-century palate, making use of some of those items which would have been difficult for most people to find during rationing. In doing so, we have not altered the nutritional content very much, but we aim to appeal to the more modern palate.

Do you remember what John Bull used to look like—

before he was invited to dig for victory and so forth—

and conserve petrol and all that—

and become a Fitter Briton, etcetera, etcetera—

and go easy at meal-times and that sort of thing—

and join the Home Guard and all—

and help with the harvest and this and that—

and do spare-time work on munitions and these and those—

and lend a hand with defence works and the like—

and be a good neighbour and so on—

and go to it and everything?

Well, just look at him now!

THE ROAD TO RATIONING

"Yes we have No Bananas"

Bananas, like most other exotic
fruit, virtually disappeared from
Britain, reviving the popular song
'Yes we have no bananas'.
(IWM HU63736)

◀

Cartoon on the impact of the war
on the nation's fitness.
(Fougasse)

A healthy diet was one of the great achievements of food rationing on Britain's Home Front during the Second World War, and is one reason why those who were children at that time have far healthier eating habits than children today. For today's reader, the important thing to emphasise is that healthy eating now does not mean having to put up with shortages and a lack of variety. What it does mean is that we can learn from the approach taken during the Second World War and enjoy our food all the more as a result.

By the time the war broke out in September 1939 the British government had already been planning the distribution of food in wartime for several years. This was not a rare example of forward thinking on the part of the authorities, but rather a reflection of the lessons learned from the mistakes and failures of the First World War (1914–18). Then, government reluctance to take any action meant that supply and demand dictated food distribution in Britain; consequently, between 1914 and 1916 prices rose by about 60 per cent. Those on lower incomes went hungry and there were complaints about waste and mismanagement, hoarding, shortages and unfairness. News of food riots was suppressed; in some parts of the country local volunteers organised soup kitchens and similar schemes in the absence of any government initiatives. Eventually a Ministry of Food was established and rationing was introduced in February 1918, but it was generally too little, too late. Similarly, the Women's Land Army was created in 1917 when, it was estimated, the country had only enough stores remaining to feed the nation for three weeks.

So in 1936, as war clouds gathered over Europe for the second time in twenty years, the government set up the Food (Defence Plans) Department. It began by stockpiling sugar and wheat, while making preparations for a national rationing scheme.

As a heavily populated but geographically small island, Britain, then as now, consumed far more food than it could produce: for instance, we produced only 20 per cent of the bacon we ate, the bulk of the rest coming from Denmark, Eire, Canada and the Baltic states. Other foods, such as bananas, could not be produced commercially here, owing to the climate. In the years leading up to the Second World War Britain imported twenty million tons of foodstuffs costing £400 million annually (the equivalent of £1.2 billion today).

It was obvious to all that Merchant Navy ships carrying food would be the focus of enemy action. Britain's reliance on food imports meant that if those ships were stopped from bringing food into the country, shortages would lead to civil unrest as they had twenty years before. If this pressure could be kept up, the nation would starve and be forced to capitulate. Rationing, it was quite clear, would be essential.

▶

An early Ministry of Food poster
encouraging people to cut down on imported foods.
(NA Image Library INF 13/143 (9))

Let your SHOPPING help our SHIPPING

PLAN YOUR MEALS TO AVOID WASTE

The government encouraged individuals to set up their own food stores. On 2 February 1939 the President of the Board of Trade told Parliament: *'I see no objection to the accumulation by householders in peace time of small reserves of suitable foodstuffs equivalent to about one week's normal requirements . . . Household reserves of this kind would constitute a useful addition to the total stocks of the country.'*

Advice and training courses proliferated. Leaflets advising on home storage of food were issued as part of the country's civil defence preparations. The emphasis was on tinned food, but people were also advised to preserve stocks of essentials such as flour, tea and sugar. The Canned Foods Advisory Bureau issued **ARP Home Storage of Food,** a booklet costing five shillings, ten shillings and one pound, suggesting several lists of foods, along with menus and recipes for their use. These stores included flour, tea, cocoa, coffee, sugar, cereals, baby and invalid foods and dried fruit, to be kept in metal containers with tightly fitting lids. The booklet suggested that, in the event of war, *'the Nation would be immediately rationed with a limited supply of meat, butter, cheese, milk, flour, tea, sugar, potatoes and cereals'.*

When war broke out on 3 September 1939 the preparations stepped up a gear. Within a week the Food (Defence Plans) Department became the Ministry of Food, with W.S. Morrison as the minister in charge.

Rationing in wartime was not seen simply as a way to keep people fed so there would be no repeat of the unrest of the last war. New discoveries about nutrition meant that by the 1930s the importance of diet and health was explicit in theory, but largely untested. Government scientists realised that the circumstances provided a unique opportunity for a major social experiment and one which the First World War had shown was necessary.

During the First World War large numbers of conscripts were found to be unfit for duty because of ill-health related to poverty and, especially, malnutrition, and this led to government-backed research into the subject. In the 1930s scientists investigated the biochemical functions of vitamins and established the body's need for them. Other research demonstrated the contribution of a poor diet to the ill-health of poorer people in this country.

The food eaten by poorer children was of particular concern and interest. In 1934 the School Medical Officer for Glossop had designed a free school meal to make up the nutritional constituents missing from the normal diet of malnourished children. During the war this was reintroduced as 'the Glossop Sandwich' or 'the Glossop Health Sandwich'. It consisted of:

- 1 pint of milk and 1 orange (when obtainable)
- If no fruit then $1/4$oz of chopped parsley included in the sandwich filling
- 3oz wholemeal bread
- $3/4$oz of butter or 'vitaminised' margarine
- $3/4$oz of salad; mustard and cress or watercress, or lettuce and tomato or carrot
- $1 1/2$oz of either cheese, salmon, herring, sardine or liver
- $3/16$oz of brewers' yeast

Early in the Second World War there were plans to feed the nation a 'basal' diet. This was worked out by nutritionists to ensure that everyone received the basic nutritional intake essential for their needs. This basal diet was to consist of 1lb of potatoes, 12oz of bread, 6oz of vegetables, 2oz of oatmeal, 1oz of fat and just over half a pint of milk per day – and no meat. The idea was that this would form the basis of a person's daily food intake and other items would be surplus to their nutritional requirements, though the need for some added flavour might make them essential.

In 1940 the plan was vetoed by the new Prime Minister, Winston Churchill, who enjoyed his food. Appalled at the idea of such a spartan approach, he wrote to the new Minister of Food, Lord Woolton: *'The way to lose the war is to try to force the British public into a diet of milk, oatmeal, potatoes etc. washed down on gala occasions with a little lime juice.'*

The wartime diet was not as stringent as Churchill feared, especially as campaigns to encourage people to grow their own food gathered pace and the convoys bringing food from Canada and the United States also carried new types of food such as Spam and soya flour. For many people the problem was more to do with the lack of variety. A long list of items remained unobtainable for much of the time, many of which we take for granted today, such as lemons and other citrus fruits, fish and imported spices.

The government's scientists, though experts in their field, were not necessarily always able to appreciate the need to make their ideas acceptable for the general population. Not that they were entirely insensitive to the views of the public. Magnus Pyke, then a government food specialist, later recalled a proposal that the government should encourage people to eat their pets. Thankfully, the plan was never pursued as the effect on the nation's morale would, it was decided, far outweigh the nutritional benefits from eating one's cat or dog. Nevertheless, the basal diet influenced a lot of scientific thinking and so the nation benefited from a diet which was nutritionally ahead of its time.

RATIONING IN THE SECOND WORLD WAR

The Women's Land Army carried out the whole range of farm work including looking after poultry.
(IWM COL 1567)

At the outbreak of the Second World War the Ministry of Food introduced price controls for essentials. Within days the first list of foods with maximum retail prices was published, and this covered eggs, butter, condensed milk, flour, sugar, tinned salmon, potatoes and dried fruits. Private purchasing of foodstuffs from abroad was prohibited and the ministry became the biggest buying organisation in the world, bulk-buying basic foods in order to keep prices down.

On 29 September 1939 the entire nation was registered and over the next few days every man, woman and child in the country was issued with an identity card. The information gathered at this point, and the card itself, would, from November, be used to issue ration books. Different-coloured ration books were issued according to circumstances and age. Adolescents, for instance, had blue books and were allocated extra meat.

On 29 November it was announced that the rationing of bacon (including ham) and butter would begin on 8 January 1940. Opposition to the announcement came from both sides of the political spectrum. Many on the left wanted to see rationing brought in immediately, and on a far wider scale than just bacon and butter, to combat the already increasing shortages and price rises. On the political right the *Daily Express* declared:

We don't need food rationing at all. It is absolute nonsense. It gives the people a sense of insecurity. It makes them feel that their supplies are unreliable. . . . Give the workman in the factory, the labourer in the fields, the soldier, the sailor and the airman all the butter and bacon they want. And ask the office worker to do without. Ask him to give up bacon altogether, and he will do so. Ask him to cut down his butter consumption, too, and watch the response. Impose rationing on him, and he will eat up his four ounces a week, to the last scrap of bacon, and the last morsel he can scrape from the butter dish.

But in general people welcomed rationing as it showed that one mistake made in the previous war would not be repeated. It was announced that as well as being rationed all butter would be pooled, and only one type, 'National Butter', would be available. Pooling sprang from the ministry's bulk-buying; the plan was that all trade brands of the most vital foods – tea, margarine, butter, dried fruits and meat paste – would disappear, to be replaced by a single National or Pool brand, to ensure consistent supplies.

There was some grumbling when a standard margarine appeared in the shops, although from February 1940 it had added vitamins A

▶

Under the Ministry of Food's milk restriction scheme, children were the first priority in the distribution of milk. This caused some resentment, but the ministry was adamant that the health of children should come first when distributing supplies.
(IWM PST 4944)

MILK THE BACKBONE OF YOUNG BRITAIN

and D, but there was major opposition when a single brand of pooled tea was mooted. Britons were far too keen on their favourite brands to put up with this bureaucratic outrage. The idea was soon dropped.

At first, butter and bacon (including ham) were rationed at 4oz a week per person, and soon after sugar, at 12oz, was added to the list. Meat came next, although this was done by cost, not weight. Each person could have 1/10*d* (9p) worth of meat a week.

The ration did not include offal, which included liver, kidneys and heart, and products such as sausages, although some offal was rationed later.

These non-rationed items were seized upon and soon became difficult to obtain. They were often supplied 'under the counter' by shopkeepers who kept them for their preferred customers.

Under-the-counter trading was viewed in very different ways by men and women. According to *Croydon Courageous:*

Men were annoyed when they could not get cigarettes and tobacco without pandering to the under-the-counter system. Women were more subtle. They often sacrificed their sweets coupons to give little tit-bits to the shop assistants and were rewarded by receiving a few of the things they needed – from under the counter, of course.

Buying rationed foods meant first registering with a local butcher, grocer and so on, and you could only buy rationed goods from them. Shops were allocated enough rations for their registered customers. When you bought your food, you had to hand over the appropriate coupons. Shopkeepers had to count the coupons and send them in to the Ministry of Food as a check against the amounts of rationed goods with which they were supplied.

In addition to organising price control and rationing, the Ministry of Food began to direct the public towards alternatives to scarce items. From this small seed grew a great deal of its later work. Public information, including recipes, hints and suggestions, formed the basis of *Food Facts* published in newspapers and periodicals; *Food Flashes* – short films shown at the cinema; and *The Kitchen Front* radio programmes, broadcast every morning.

This grocer is selling National Butter and the 'Special Margarine' with added vitamins.
(IWM D2373)

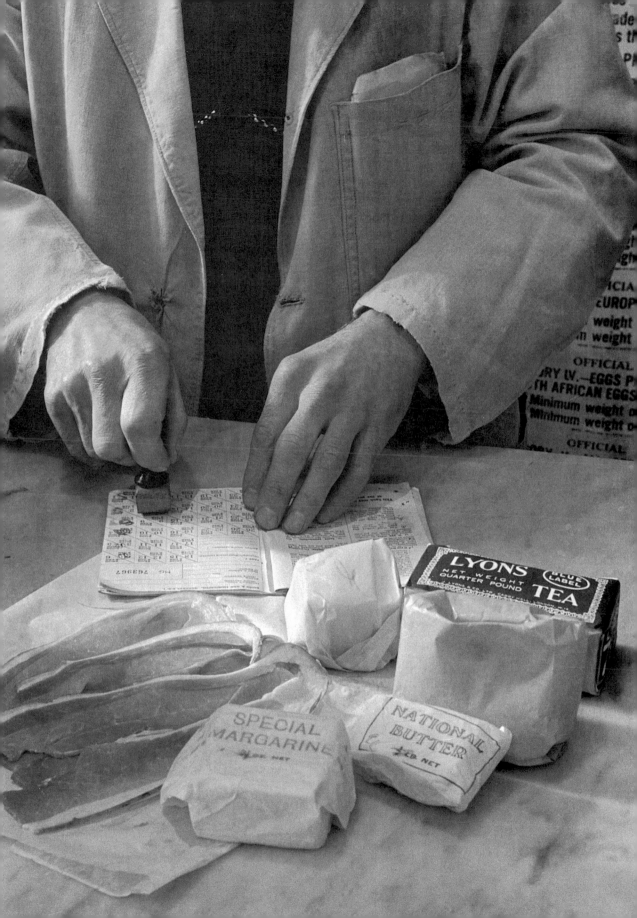

FOODS
AND
HOW TO PREPA
WITH 150 MEA
KITCHEN PARA
(A HURRICANE B
DAY-TO-DAY
MENUS
FOR A
PRACTICAL!
APPETISING!
YOUR RAT
SOLVED b
I. D
AU

FOOD
FACTS
OR T
T

COOKIN
in
WAR-TIME
Elizabeth Craig

On 3 April 1940 Morrison was replaced by Frederick Marquis, 1st Baron Woolton. He was a well-known businessman, who had spent part of his early working life as a social worker in Liverpool. Many saw the post as a poisoned chalice, but Lord Woolton was remarkably successful and was held in some affection by the public as he travelled round the country, giving talks and supporting cookery demonstrations. Woolton saw his job as more than just ensuring fair shares. He later wrote: *'I determined to use the powers I possessed to stamp out the diseases that arose from malnutrition, especially those amongst children, such as rickets.'*

On 1 July 1940 he launched the National Milk Scheme, his first attack on 'the diseases that arose from malnutrition'. The idea was to encourage children under five to drink more milk, by providing a pint of milk a day for each child, either for 2*d* (1p) a pint or for free, depending on the family's financial circumstances. The same applied to expectant and nursing mothers.

After these groups had received their milk, what remained was shared equally among the rest of each supplier's customers; this averaged about 3 pints a week each. Consumers had to register with a milk supplier, usually the milkman who delivered to their road. To save fuel and manpower, each area was divided up between the various dairies so each had a monopoly on delivery to specified streets. Fuel rationing meant that later on in the war deliveries were further restricted; bread could only be delivered every other day, and milk only once a day. Suppliers got together and pooled deliveries, so that the butcher might also deliver bread, fish and other groceries.

In December 1941 points rationing was introduced. Certain goods were in very short supply and this meant that they could not be rationed; the Ministry of Food was only prepared to ration goods if it could guarantee that everyone would receive their supply each week. There were many reasons, such as insufficient supply or high seasonal fluctuations, which precluded goods from rationing. The points scheme solved this problem. On top of basic rations, each person received points coupons which they could use in any shop on a range of shortage items, which each had their own points value.

The Ministry of Food produced lots of advice for the housewife, much of it in the form of leaflets such as this one, which advocated quick boiling in a little water to retain the goodness of cabbage.
(Crown Copyright)

Try cooking Cabbage this way

LID TIGHTLY ON COOK FOR 10-15 MINUTES

CABBAGE SHREDDED COARSELY

JUST ENOUGH WATER TO COVER BOTTOM OF PAN

It's twice as delicious

Coupons were allocated monthly and could be redeemed at any time during that month.

To get the scheme off to a good start the ministry built up a stock of points goods in the shops. A 'stop sale' order was put on canned meats, beans and fish, the first goods to be included in the scheme, and a further 30,000 tons were issued from government stocks. So when the points scheme started,

Lord Woolton, Minister of Food from April 1940 to November 1943, was one of the more high-profile, and well-loved, members of the wartime cabinet. 'Those who have the will to win eat potatoes in their skin, knowing that the sight of peelings deeply hurts Lord Woolton's feelings', went the wartime verse. (IWM HU48187)

▶

As with most good intentions, the real problem was not to get people started but to keep them going; thus the 'Dig for Victory' campaign became the 'Dig On for Victory' campaign. (Crown Copyright)

items appeared in the shops which had not been available for weeks or even months, and this made it an instant success.

The other advantage of the scheme was that the customer became a shopper again, able to choose what he or she bought. The great advantage to the ministry was that the scheme was very responsive to supply and demand; if stocks of particular goods on points began to run low, the ministry had simply to raise their points value, discouraging consumption. On the other hand, goods of which there was a surfeit could have their points value reduced.

By this time 'Dig for Victory', introduced in 1939, and its successor, 'Dig On for Victory', had really taken off. These campaigns ensured that just about every piece of land, private or public, was turned over to growing fruit and vegetables. The national diet was now heavily dependent on home-grown produce. Consumption of meat, fish, poultry, oils and fats had been reduced in favour of home-grown cereals and vegetables. Cereals and potatoes made up just about half the national diet.

Potatoes, rich in vitamin C and carbohydrate, grew easily in Britain, and became central to the ministry's plans. In 1937 Britain had imported almost a quarter of a million tons of potatoes but by 1940 we were self-sufficient. However, the ministry was not satisfied; figures showed that the average Briton ate only ½lb per head daily – only half the amount consumed in Ireland. The minister set a target of ¾lb per person per day. Potato Pete, a cartoon character who appeared on posters and cookery books, was created by the Ministry of Food to encourage people to eat more potatoes. It certainly worked; by the end of the war potato consumption had been raised by 60 per cent.

Onions were another success story. Traditionally imported from Brittany, the Channel Islands and Spain, onions became scarce after the fall of France in 1940. At this time onions were often given as raffle prizes or as very welcome presents. However, by 1941 the worst of these shortages were over, as the Ministry of Agriculture announced a fifteen-fold increase in domestic production. This did not altogether wipe out shortages, and from September 1941 the

▼

Buying provisions in a typical wartime grocer's shop. Notice the classic shopping basket, the powdered egg and the WI (Women's Institute) bottled produce, and the assistant marking off purchases in the ration book. (IWM D17518)

▶

Potato Pete was an early cartoon character used to encourage people to eat more potatoes. This is Potato Pete's recipe book, suggesting all sorts of ways to prepare them. (Crown Copyright)

Potato Pete's recipe book

ministry introduced an Onion Distribution Scheme. But by 1944 supply exceeded demand and the scheme was no longer needed.

Eggs were rarely plentiful at national level although some people had good supplies locally. At the start of the war a shortage of poultry feed, which was imported, had led to a shortage of eggs; by April 1940 there was only enough feed for about one-sixth of the birds kept in 1939. In June a scheme for the control and distribution of eggs was brought in. Egg supplies were equally distributed through-out the country and retailers were told to allocate them fairly to their customers; this often meant that you might receive only one egg a week, or even three a month. In 1942 each registered customer received twenty-nine eggs, in 1943 thirty and in the first three months of 1944 just four. Imported dried eggs, introduced in 1942, were an essential and generally popular alternative.

▼

Tommy Handley cartoon, counting coupons.
(*Radio Fun* comic)

" I must say I rather like this beige bread."

The National Loaf, made from high-fibre wheatmeal flour, was not one of the Ministry of Food's greatest successes. For many years white bread had been successfully marketed as higher class than 'peasant' brown bread. (*Sillince*)

This mobile emergency shop was used by Sainsbury's to replace temporarily any of their stores put out of action by the bombing until the regular premises could reopen for business. (IWM HU63812)

SAVE KITCHEN SCRAPS TO FEED THE HENS!

KITCHEN WASTE

KEEP IT DRY, FREE FROM GLASS, METAL, BONES, PAPER, ETC. IT ALSO FEEDS PIGS...... YOUR COUNCIL WILL COLLECT.

PRINTED FOR H.M. STATIONERY OFFICE BY H. MANLY & SON LTD. 51-2333 S.P.56.

Another healthy but on the whole unwelcome development was National Wheatmeal Flour, introduced in 1941. This used more of the wheat than white flour. One year later Lord Woolton announced that all flour would henceforward be of the wheatmeal variety. Production of existing brands of wholemeal bread such as Hovis and Allinsons continued, but white bread could be made only under special licence. The immediate consequence was the introduction of the National Loaf which had an unusual texture and did not keep well so although it was much healthier, it was not generally popular.

The year 1942 also saw the introduction of rationing for sweets and chocolate. At first each person could buy 8oz a month; on 23 August this was increased to 16oz, then it fell back to 12oz on 18 October, where it remained.

In August 1942 the sugar ration was drastically reduced, from 1lb to 8oz. Biscuits were placed on points, as were syrup and treacle; fats now became a separately rationed item – 8oz in total, with no more than 2oz of this being butter – while 2d (1p) of the meat ration now had to be taken in corned beef.

By 1944 the Ministry of Food recognised that much of the nation's food had become bland. In an advert that April they recommended that you:

Grow your own flavourings. Herbs are such a boon in varying the flavour of soups, stews and salads, that it pays to have some always by you. . . . Mint, chives (the spiky green leaves of which taste like spring onion), sage, thyme, parsley. Parsley, indeed, is an important health-protector too; it is so rich in vitamin C and in iron. You need very little ground – sunny window boxes or a few pots will do. Now is the time to plant. And don't forget to dry some of your herb harvest for winter use.

As rationing went on the shortage of meat encouraged alternatives; rabbit was widely used, and sausages contained less and less real meat: *'It's a mystery what's in these sausages,'* says a character in the 1943 film **Millions Like Us**, *'and I hope its not solved in my time!'*

By that year horsemeat, or horse flesh as it was known, was commonly available. Most people disliked the idea, but many housewives served it to their families without revealing what it was. On the other hand, whale meat, which became available in 1945, was widely

◀ ────────────

Nothing was wasted. Kitchen scraps were recycled
for animal feed.
(IWM HU63812)

hated for its fishy, oily taste. Tinned meat was imported from the United States, and in this way Spam (chopped pork luncheon meat) entered the national diet. Corned beef too was regularly on the menu.

The end of the war did not mean the end of rationing. As the country struggled to pay off its debts and support postwar reconstruction, shortages actually increased. Rationing of some staple foods got worse; bread was rationed in July 1946 and potatoes from December 1947. Generally, more and more items were, if not freely available, unrationed. But it was a slow process and it was not until 1954, nearly ten years after the war ended, that the ration book was finally abandoned.

This picture dates from the first egg shortages, hence the Bird's Egg Powder, and the various 'I-T' mixtures announcing 'no eggs required'. Some of the other goods on sale would soon become very scarce. (IWM D2374)

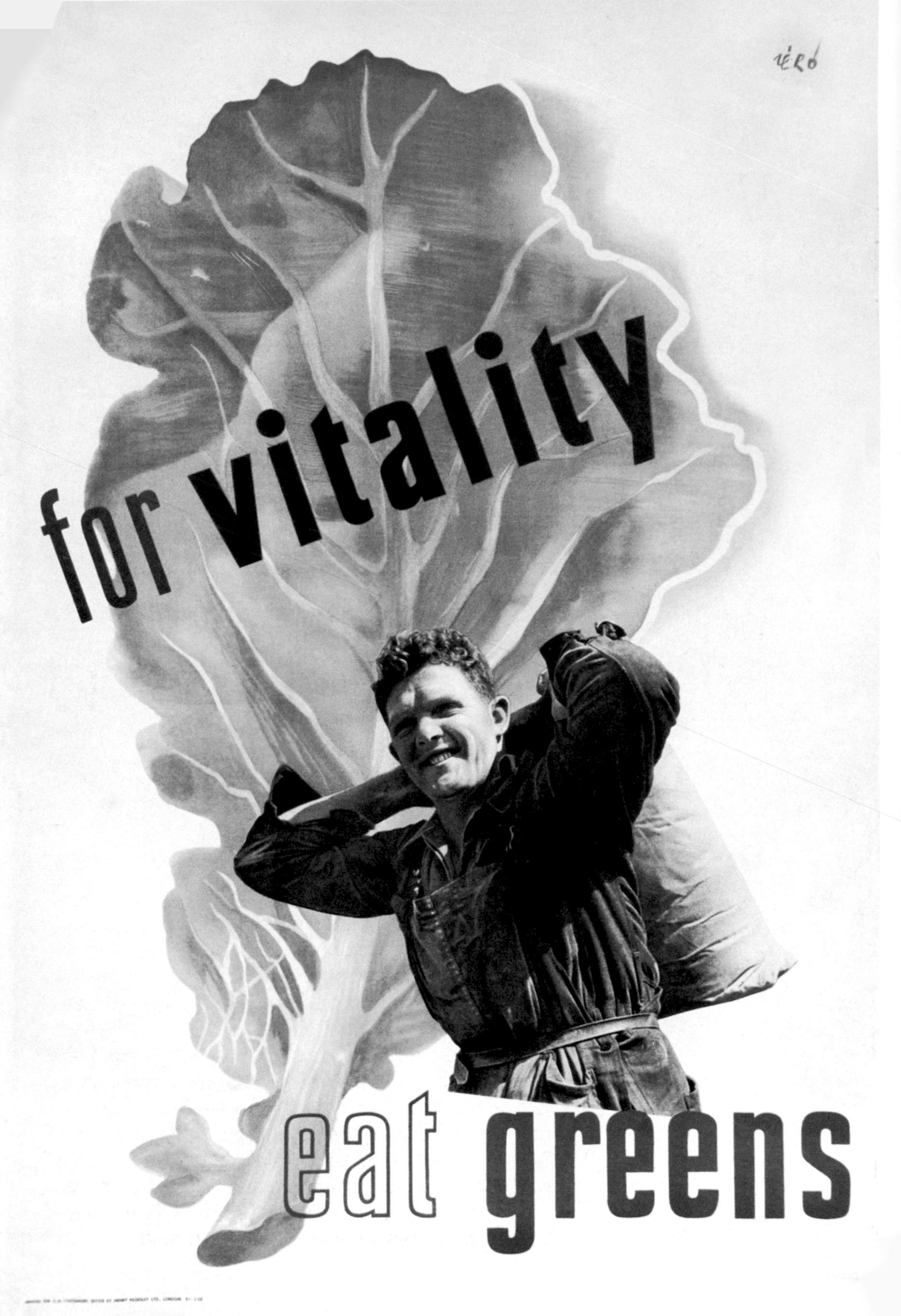
for vitality
eat greens

Using the Wartime Diet Today

Rationing was an essential part of fighting the war on the Home Front. It meant that the nation had enough food to go round and that people were fit enough to play their part in a war which, uniquely for this country, involved the whole population, civilian and military. In contrast to pre-war Britain, married women were no longer based at home looking after their offspring and their husbands. Everyone had a job to do. This was essential to keep the country running, producing enough food, munitions and other wartime essentials, as well as looking after evacuees, doing civil defence duties or other additional work. And when you finally finished work for the day, there was always the vegetable plot to tend.

With its emphasis on fresh fruit and vegetables, and limited quantities of meat, fat, sugar and dairy products, the wartime diet was very healthy and certainly provided enough energy and vitamins to keep people fit and healthy. Cookery books and leaflets emphasising the healthy aspects of the diet proliferated, from the Ministry of Food and other sources. Well-known chefs wrote books, and gave demonstrations and lessons on cooking; so too did groups such as the Women's Institute and the Women's Voluntary Services.

Polish women refugees for example, produced a very useful cookery book which included a wide range of warming and filling recipes largely based on cabbage and related vegetables.

Wartime cookery books reflect changes in rations and the changing availability of other foodstuffs.

The written style of many of the recipes suggests that the 1940s cook would have a degree of cookery knowledge not usually found today. Modern recipe writing assumes less knowledge and more use of labour-saving devices.

Food supplies during the war fluctuated drastically; food that was easily available early on became difficult to find later while other items became far easier to obtain. Supplies such as tinned meats and Canadian salmon increased as the threat to shipping from U-boats was countered during the Battle of the Atlantic. Victories in North Africa meant that some imported foods were once again available as trade with previously enemy-occupied countries resumed. The emphasis on home-produced foods gained momentum.

People adapted their style of eating radically, reflecting these fluctuations. In 1942 the production of cereals and vegetables in England and Wales had increased by more than 50 per cent compared to the pre-war period, while the numbers of animals reared had dropped, pigs by 51 per cent and poultry by 24 per cent.

Vegetarianism grew in popularity during the 1930s but this growth declined during the war as it became known that Hitler was a vegetarian. Official records put the number of vegetarians in the UK during the Second World War at about 100,000, and they received extra cheese instead of meat.

▶

All sorts of new foods were introduced. Some, such as Icelandic salt cod, proved far from popular. Even after soaking for a day, most people found it far too salty. (IWM PST 0068)

A NEW FISH DISH

FRESH-
SALTED
COD

9D lb.

The KITCHEN FRONT

122 WARTIME RECIPES

broadcast by Frederick Grisewood, Mabel Constanduros and others, specially selected by the Ministry of Food.

6 D. NET

There were certainly fewer vegetarians then than there are today but the emphasis on vegetables and cereals and tight meat rationing meant that vegetarian recipes were enjoyed by many people who also ate meat and fish. Meat-free recipes were a common feature of the wartime diet.

Today we are inundated with options and have become used to food in abundance. This didn't apply during the war; even if you had the money to spend, there was little to spend it on and shoppers just had to make do with what was available. People filled themselves up with carbohydrate and had limited resources of meat, fats and sugar. A good, filling meal was enjoyed daily, but there were few snacks, which meant none of the crisps, fizzy drinks and sweets that are easily available today. The nearest alternative was an apple.

Rationing meant only one bar of chocolate a week, while biscuits were on points, allowing at best a small packet a week. Ready-made cakes were boring – no icing, limited sugar, no cream, a tiny amount of jam, and only a few currants in the currant buns. It is now not only possible but fairly common for people to eat on a daily basis the equivalent of one week's sweet rations (about 3oz – 85g – or one small chocolate bar). We think nothing of slapping butter on our bread, pouring cream into our coffee or on to desserts, or eating a whole bag of sweets or a hamburger, as the mood takes us. Add in the power of advertising and marketing and paradoxically, the choice makes it hard for us to make informed decisions about what is good for us and what isn't. We are surrounded by temptation.

By contrast, when rationing was announced temptation was certainly not a problem. At that time the press pointed out that the butter and bacon rations gave the equivalent of five thinly spread slices of bread a day, and four rashers a week. *The Times* recalled that in the First World War the Ministry of Food had suggested that bread and butter be eaten butter-side down. The advantage of this was that it put the butter directly on the tongue.

Making the best of the food you had meant that during the war every scrap of food had a use; wastage was avoided at all costs. Meat bones were used to make stock. A simmering stockpot with meat and vegetable trimmings, including dried onion skins, would be always on the go. Milk bottles were rinsed out with water to create 'milk-water' for use in making batters. Whole books were dedicated

Cover of the Ministry of Food recipe book,
The Kitchen Front, with illustrations by Fougasse.
(Authors' Collection)

to recipes for using up leftovers. These hardly need an added modern twist – many people still do much the same but use the microwave.

Suggestions were made to help make ingredients stretch that much further: after making your jam, for example, you were advised to boil water in the dirty saucepan, then strain it, producing a 'delicious fruit drink'. The home cook was encouraged to eke out the butter ration by incorporating milk or water into the butter. Some would mix the pooled margarine with butter to make the former taste better and the latter go further. Thankfully, we do not have to do this – the results were not always popular.

One peculiarity of the diet in early wartime was the amount of sugar it contained. Britons ate more sugar than just about any other country in Europe and initially the ration was 12oz per person per week. The amount of sugar in the diet fell steadily throughout the war.

The amount of sugar each person could have, like most rations, changed according to availability. Extra sugar was allocated at the time of fruit harvests so that people could make jam, although they were also given recipes which needed less sugar for more immediate use. These have a parallel in the lower-sugar, 'extra fruit' jams and conserves we buy today and which are kept in the fridge – not an option for many wartime households. Today, we are more aware of the need to eat less sugar, although large quantities are still added to processed food.

The 'cooking fat' often referred to in wartime was almost always saturated fat, although it was used in small quantities. Recipes would use margarine in place of butter. 'Cooking oil', made from dripping and fat rendered from bacon or cooked meats, was used for frying, as were children's supplies of cod-liver oil. Precious butter rations would be spread on bread and would only rarely be used in cooking. People were advised to divide the butter ration into individual daily portions so that it was evenly distributed through the week.

Today we can substitute healthy alternatives such as sunflower oil and olive oil for the saturated fat that was used then. This is one area where our diet has definitely improved and olive oil has become one of the most popular forms of cooking oil used in Britain. Low-fat spreads are also widely used. A healthy diet should include bread, which should be wholemeal, and spread thinly: 'spread it on and scrape it off' is the description used by one wartime child. The same goes for jam or preserves: high-fruit, low-sugar varieties are the closest we can get to wartime versions.

The main drink was tea (which was rationed), sweetened with a little sugar taken from the weekly ration, and a little milk. The sugar substitutes which were available then were not very good, but

lend a hand on the land

at a farming holiday camp

PRINTED FOR H.M.STATIONERY OFFICE BY CHROMOWORKS L™ LONDON 51– 3727

ISSUED BY THE MINISTRY OF AGRICULTURE

Housewife

AUGUST
9d
1943

OUR LIFESTYLES THEN AND NOW

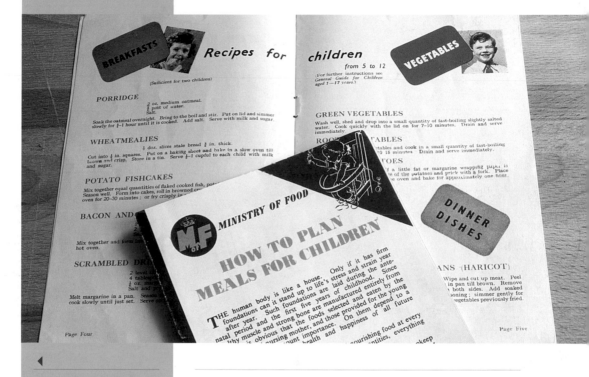

In the sixty years since the end of the war there have been many lifestyle changes. One of the most obvious differences is a vast increase in affluence. Most of us are far better off materially than our wartime predecessors, but this has not necessarily led to better health. The two most common causes of death in the United Kingdom today are heart disease and cancer. It is estimated that one-third of these deaths are linked to poor diet and are preventable. Levels of obesity are rising at a dramatic rate. In 1980 6 per cent of men and 8 per cent of women were obese; by 2000 21 per cent of men and women were obese, and there has been a massive increase in obesity among children.

Ill-health caused by a poor diet was also an issue in 1939, but for completely different reasons. Many people on low incomes were prey to diseases of malnutrition. The need to give children a healthy start in life, in mind and body, could no longer be ignored in social policy; the effects of poverty were too obvious. During the war schemes providing school milk, blackcurrant juice, orange juice and cod-liver oil were introduced to give young children a healthy start.

But despite the efforts of the government to introduce a healthier diet, in 1957 P. Inman wrote in *Labour in the Munitions Industries:*

Areas of high unemployment in the 1930s, such as Glasgow, Liverpool and Merthyr Tydfil, continued to experience lower standards of health than the rest of the country. A number of Royal Ordnance Factories were located in the 'special' or 'depressed' areas and it was thought that workers recruited from these areas were less productive because 'malnutrition was common amongst both young and old'.

During the war Ministry of Food surveys showed that large families 'still found it difficult to afford adequate meat, fish, vegetables and fruit'. Mothers particularly went without, giving their meat and vegetable portions to others in the family and filling up on bread and cakes. But the extensive research carried out at the time showed that from 1942 the health of the nation improved. In *Health and Society in Twentieth Century Britain*, Helen Jones said, 'For many people there were definite signs of improved health in the later stages of the war, and this is closely linked to rising standards of living.'

Exercise is another major difference in our lifestyle. Today, exercise is something we opt to take. During the war and for some time afterwards, it was part of daily living. In the 1930s cars were still comparatively expensive, so private ownership was restricted to the better-off. With the advent of war petrol was heavily rationed, and the majority got around by means of public transport, cycling and walking. Even the use of public transport was frowned upon; the government urged people not to travel, asking, in the words of Bert Thomas's famous poster, 'Is your journey really necessary?' One wartime publication said that everyone would be healthier and happier for walking 8 miles a day, slightly more than the 10,000 steps we are recommended to take nowadays.

Many experts recommended gardening. This made a virtue of the necessity to encourage people to grow their own food. In 1942 there were more than 1.5 million allotments in Britain – nearly twice the pre-war level – and there were many more people who grew food in their gardens.

That said, many people were unfit, but in contrast to today this was more to do with being underfed rather than obese, or with living in damp and polluted environments, especially in cities choked with smoke from coal fires, railways and factory chimneys.

The Ministry of Health worked hard to change the nation's eating habits. Before the war the nation's diet had consisted of meat-intensive meals, and stodgy puddings. Now expediency dictated a diet containing far less meat and far more fresh vegetables. Along with campaigns encouraging people to grow their own food went campaigns explaining the health benefits of a diet rich in fresh produce. *Good Food in Wartime*, published by the Board of Education in 1941, said, 'Salads and vegetables (both green and root) should be served regularly during the winter months as they give protection against colds and other ills then prevalent.' A Ministry of Food advert from 1943 went even further:

Salads are nature's tonics and beauty foods. They put a sparkle in the eyes, gloss on the hair and spring in the step. They're doubly important now; they have not only to play their own good part, but take the place of fruit as well. A salad a day should be your rule; a good big plateful, not just a finicky spoonful or so!

Drinking water was advised: 'water flushes the kidneys, corrects skin dryness, and helps to cure constipation . . . Most people benefit by taking a glass of water first thing in the morning and last thing at night – if the skin is spotty, take it hot.' Of course, water came from the tap; in wartime Britain no one had heard of the bottled varieties, but the advice was as true then as it is now.

A major difference between the wartime diet and today's is the availability of ready-made and fast food. This reflects the influence of the USA on post-war lifestyles. War-torn Europe looked to America as a land of abundance. Hamburgers and cola were an affordable and increasingly accessible way to buy into this lifestyle.

With its aggressive marketing campaigns aimed largely at children, McDonalds is now the standard by which many children judge other food. Takeaway food, including high-fat fried chicken and pizzas, have become part of daily life, as have sweets and crisps, high in fat and low in nutritional value. In 2002 Sodexho surveyed 8–16 year olds. It found that the most popular foods were 'hand-held' items such as pizza, burgers, fruit and sandwiches. A further finding indicates a huge increase in 'snacking'; it showed that children spent £433 million on food and drink going to and from school. This went mostly on sweets, then crisps, chocolate and fizzy drinks.

Technology has changed the way we eat. Family meals round the table were the norm in the 1940s, starting with a good breakfast. Breakfast in the fullest sense was similar to today's, consisting of porridge, toast and/or cereal, bacon, fruit, smoked fish such as kippers, and/or eggs. Bacon was

SAVE BREAD

and you save lives

SERVE

POTATOES

& you serve the country

PRINTED FOR H.M. STATIONERY OFFICE BY JAMES HAWORTH & BROTHER, LTD., LONDON. 51-2884

probably more popular then than now and many breakfast dishes such as kedgeree were prepared the night before and heated in the morning. Now more and more adults and, more worryingly, children, are skipping breakfast. The 2002 Sodexho survey showed that 8 per cent of British children had nothing to eat before school, rising to 18 per cent for 15–16-year-old boys and 21 per cent for girls of the same age.

In many households during the 1930s a substantial meal prepared by the woman of the house would be eaten at midday by the whole family, with children and adults working nearby coming home during the day. It would have a main course and a dessert or sweet, followed by cheese and biscuits, and tea or coffee.

By the middle of the war, with much of the nation involved in war work, going home for lunch was no longer a habit of the majority. From 1940 onwards the government encouraged the provision of factory canteens to ensure that workers had a main meal every day at a reasonable price. In the spring of 1942 school meals were introduced to provide children with a nourishing midday meal. Each child received 2 pennyworth of meat each day – twice as much as was issued to adults in British Restaurants. By 1943 schools were providing meals for 750,000 children.

In the 1930s teatime would be sandwiches and cake, while supper would be a light cooked meal such as cauliflower cheese or, particularly for children, bread soaked in warm milk. During the war, especially following conscription, most women were out at work all day so the style of food became quick, simple, and cost and ration effective. Frozen and dried foods were the results of government research into transporting and storing food, and their convenience made them more popular. Snacks such as cheese on toast or meals in works canteens and communal restaurants were part of a wartime trend for eating out, something we do increasingly today for pleasure rather than practical purposes.

Today, convenience foods and microwave ovens mean we spend much of our time eating individual meals sitting in front of the television. Watching the TV has become a national pastime, taking the place of outdoor pursuits, and adding to our low levels of fitness – remember that during the war there was no television. Over the past fifty years we have embraced new ideas and trends, partly as a result of growing cultural diversity and wider travel.

Shipping food into the country cost lives, so eating home-grown food, such as potatoes, was regarded as a patriotic duty. (IWM PST 0743)

On 8 December 1941 the Vitamin Welfare Scheme was initiated to counter malnutrition in the young. Babies, young children, expectant and nursing mothers received Lend-lease orange juice, cod-liver oil, blackcurrant puree and extra milk through the welfare system. (IWM V164)

The chip shop, the only takeaway food outlet of the 1940s, now competes with restaurants selling Chinese, Indian, Thai, Mexican and other ethnically defined food, and of course there are the ubiquitous pizzas and kebabs.

Shopping today is very different. Today we do at least a week's shopping in the supermarket, where we get nearly all our food. In spite of this we tend to live day by day with minimal planning for the week ahead. During the 1940s the way of life was one week at a time, making it much easier to plan a diet. Shopping was done daily in different outlets – the butcher, the grocer, the fishmonger, the milkman, and so on – and most shops delivered. Home freezers were unheard of and refrigerators far from standard.

The war had one special feature in terms of shopping: the queue. When shops obtained anything a little unusual, or any shortage item, a queue soon formed outside. Bessie Palmer, a housewife during the war, remembers: 'You saw a queue, you joined it. You got on the end of it and you might come back with one orange. You stood in the queue, and as people came along, you asked, "What are they selling?" Whenever there was a queue, somebody would pass the message on; there's a queue down so-and-so.'

Although the main components of the British diet are the same, what has changed is how we put them together and what we add to them. The British diet is still basically bread, milk, meat and potatoes, but it is relatively low in fruit and vegetables compared to wartime, and we're eating less fish now than we did. This is a concern as we now know that oily fish is a rich source of Omega-3, which is good for just about everything.

Tea was the most common drink for children but today children drink two-thirds more fizzy drinks than milk (National Diet and Nutrition Survey). However, when we do drink milk, it is more often skimmed or semi-skimmed than whole milk.

We eat roughly the same amount of cheese and cream as we used to, but since it became widely available in the 1970s, yoghurt has been increasingly popular. We now eat less than half the number of eggs we did.

When beef, lamb, pork, ham and bacon were taken off the ration, people at first ate a lot more of them. Since the 1950s we have begun to eat less and less meat, and the number of vegetarians has risen sharply. In addition, a large proportion of the population avoids red meat for a healthier diet. This is one reason why chicken and turkey have increased steadily in popularity to the point where we now eat as much poultry as beef, lamb and pork put together.

Fats and sugars were a significant part of the British diet leading up to the war. Until the 1980s we consumed a weekly average of 300g of spreading and cooking fats, and oils. Since then this has dropped to around 186g. Olive oil, a healthy alternative to the saturated fats of fifty years ago, is now a common ingredient in cooking. But we eat quite high levels of 'hidden' fats in cakes, biscuits and convenience foods.

The wartime National Loaf, with its high wheatmeal content, was never popular. Immediately after the war people enthusiastically went back to white bread, and brown bread continued to be regarded as inferior for many years. Today, although white bread is still the most popular, we eat more brown, wholemeal and other types of breads.

Despite the fact that fresh vegetables especially are packed with vitamins, minerals and fibre, consumption has continued to decline. We buy fewer traditional British greens and root vegetables and instead we're turning to fresh imports, such as courgettes and corn on the cob, and frozen exotic vegetables such as mange-tout. However, we're eating more fresh fruit than we did. More exotic varieties and imports have increased choice at the shops, while tinned fruit has become less popular.

Despite all the additional knowledge and experience we have gained during and since the war, our choices are not particularly well-informed. But there are encouraging signs: healthy eating is seen increasingly as an important part of everyday life and not just something to do when we go on a diet to lose weight. And there is growing awareness that that means buying good, fresh food, not the overpriced and over-prepared foods often labelled 'healthy' at the supermarkets.

◀

Hoarding was always frowned upon although people were advised to keep an emergency store of food. In March 1942 it became illegal to hoard more than four weeks' supply of un-rationed foodstuffs. This shows the store permitted for a family of four at that time.
(IWM V110)

HOW THE RECIPES WORK

The Radio doctor says . . .

An ounce of cabbage is worth an inch of lipstick!

MINISTRY OF FOOD

A Ministry of Food poster, typical of the sort seen inside buses of the period. The ministry worked hard to get people to eat healthily.
(Crown Copyright)

Using seasonal produce and a basic ration of meat, fats and sugar, we have chosen a selection of dishes that would have been cooked during the war. The original recipes come from various sources and many reflect the written style of that time. For authenticity, we have left these recipes in their original form. There were many respected cookery writers at work during the war, all of whom contributed immeasurably to morale on the kitchen front.

In addition, we have devised modern recipes. Dishes have been created that can be used over the period of a week using the rations that would have been available in wartime. Food rationing fluctuated according to the availability of raw materials, so to be as accurate as possible we have divided the book into seasons and created recipes suitable for the rationed foodstuffs to hand at that time of year.

The recipes are a combination of traditional and modern, using basic ingredients, methods of cooking and recipe styles from the 1940s and today. We have included some original wartime meals and have devised others to reflect the wide variety of choice and tastes of the twenty-first century.

NUTRITIONAL VALUES

We asked a nutritionist to calculate the kcals, protein, fats (including saturated fat), carbohydrate, total sugars and fibre content of each recipe given. These calculations can be found after each recipe, both wartime and modern, and are noted in metric only.

FOODS FOR SPRING

Another variation on the theme of eating potatoes. Not only patriotic but healthy.
(IWM PST 3366)

In the spring of 1940 rationing had just started and effects were beginning to be felt. Stores of winter root vegetables and young spring vegetables along with new potatoes, easy-to-grow rhubarb, gooseberries, broad beans, young peas and the luxury asparagus were all on the menu, as were spring greens and mint, one of the earliest herbs to appear.

Spring

Both the wartime and modern recipes for spring rely on stores of root and tuber crops that have kept well during the winter. They include carrots and potatoes, along with store cupboard essentials like dried fruits for a compote. We use herbs such as sage and rosemary that will have kept going through the winter, and offerings like broad beans and asparagus from a late spring garden. As the weather at this time of year swings from warm and hopeful to windy, damp and chilly, our recipe selection offers warming meals and light dishes for those days when it feels as though summer is on its way.

wartime recipes	modern recipes
Stewed Ox cheek	Oxtail and ale casserole
Nettle champ	Young spinach and spring onion champ
Rhubarb bread pudding	Layered rhubarb fool
Mixed vegetable curry	Ham and pickle pie
Casserole of fresh fish	Mixed bitter leaf salad
Herring and horseradish paste	Spicy spring vegetable sauté
Apricot compote	Kidneys with mustard and maderia
Porridge scones	Vinegar and mustard baked chicken
	Monkfish, bacon and sage casserole
	Broad beans with minted salsa verde
	Fig, apricot and date compote with star anise
	Oatmeal scones
	Carrot and ginger marmalade

A WEEKLY MENU IN SPRING

Sunday	Oxtail and Ale Casserole
	Young Spinach and Spring Onion Champ
	Layered Rhubarb Fool
Monday	Ham and Pickle Pie
	Mixed Bitter Leaf and Seed Salad
Tuesday	Spicy Spring Vegetable Sauté
Wednesday	Kidneys with Mustard and Madeira Gravy
Thursday	Vinegar and Mustard Baked Chicken
Friday	Monkfish, Bacon and Sage Casserole
Saturday Lunch	Sardine, Horseradish and Chive Pâté
	Broad Beans with Minted Salsa Verde
	Fig, Apricot and Date Compote with Star Anise
Treat of the Week	Oatmeal Scones with Carrot and Ginger Marmalade

Meat Rations and Cuts of Meat

With meat rationed by cost, not by weight, cheaper cuts were the order of the day, as this stretched the ration to feed a family. Wartime publications advised extensively on methods of cooking less expensive cuts of meat, including brisket (breast of beef), salt beef, shin and mince, mutton, rabbit, veal, venison and 'not-so-young' chickens. Offal was popular as it was not generally rationed. Cuts included sheep's head, tripe, hearts, brains, cow heel, ox cheek, trotters and brawn as well as kidneys and liver.

Stewed Ox Cheek   Serves 4–6 (taken from *Food Facts for the Kitchen Front*)

Ox cheek has today returned to some menus, mainly in fashionable restaurants. Its popularity is not really surprising as long hours of slow cooking produce a rich, meltingly tender casserole.

INGREDIENTS

1 ox cheek	1 parsnip
2 or 3 carrots	1 small turnip
A bunch of herbs	1oz (30g) margarine
1oz (30g) flour	Salt and pepper

METHOD

Wash the cheek well in warm water, then put in a saucepan, cover with cold water, bring to the boil and skim thoroughly. Add the vegetables, sliced, and the herbs and seasoning. Stew very slowly, keeping just enough liquid in the pan to cover, for 3 to 4 hours, or until the bones come away from the cheek easily.

Melt the margarine in a pan, mix in the flour smoothly, cook for 2 or 3 minutes, then add slowly 1 pint of the liquid from the pan and bring to the boil, stirring all the time. Season if necessary.

Remove the bones from the meat, pour on the sauce and simmer together for 10 minutes before serving.

NUTRITIONAL VALUE
(assuming one ox cheek weighs 200g)
190 cals
13g protein
9g fat

1g saturated fat
15g carbohydrate
7g total sugars
3g fibre

And now...   Ox cheek may be obtained from some butchers. Similarly, ox tail is tasty, readily available and regaining popularity.

Oxtail and Ale Casserole   Serves 4–5

Take 2 oxtails, trimmed and cut into joints. Roll each piece in flour seasoned with salt, pepper and paprika. Brown the oxtails in 1tbsp hot oil in a large casserole. Lift out on to a plate. Add 2 large thinly sliced onions to the casserole along with 1tbsp soft dark brown sugar. Cook over a low heat for 12–15 minutes or until soft. Replace the oxtails and pour over 450ml (3/4 pint) brown stock and 600ml (1 pint) ale. Add 4–5 sprigs of thyme and a bay leaf. Bring to the boil, cover and cook for 2½–3 hours at 150°C or until the oxtails are tender. Once cooked, lift them on to a plate, skim the cooking liquid of excess fat and reduce to a sticky consistency by boiling rapidly. Replace the oxtails and season to taste. Serve with mashed potatoes.

NUTRITIONAL VALUE
534 cals
23g protein
13g fat

5g saturated fat
22g carbohydrate
16g total sugars
1g fibre

Nettle Champ   (taken from *Food Facts for the Kitchen Front*)

This recipe incorporates young spring nettle leaves, freely available in local hedgerows, parks and fields.

INGREDIENTS

2lb (900g) potatoes

1oz (30g) margarine or dripping

A little milk

Nettles, spring onions or cabbage, according to season

METHOD

Cook a large pan of potatoes, allowing them to steam off and dry in the usual way. Cook the selected vegetable in a very little water (with the lid on). Peel and mash the potatoes, beating well, then pour in a little milk, add seasoning of pepper and salt, then the cooked vegetable. Serve piping hot on hot plates, with a small pat of margarine or dripping on each portion.

NUTRITIONAL VALUE
(assuming 900g potatoes and
30g dripping)
237 cals
6g protein

7g fat
0.5g saturated fat
40g carbohydrate
3g total sugars
3g fibre

And now...   Nettles are excellent simply wilted in a little oil or pureed in soups, but you need to pick them when they are still young. Young spinach leaves or rocket and spring onions make a great version of the traditional Irish champ.

Young Spinach and Spring Onion Champ   Serves 4

Cook and mash 900g (2lb) potatoes with 30g (1oz) butter and a splash of skimmed milk. Season with salt, pepper and nutmeg. Stir in a handful of washed baby spinach leaves and 4 finely sliced spring onions along with 4 tbsp Greek yoghurt. Serve straightaway.

NUTRITIONAL VALUE
245 cals
6g protein
8g fat

0.6g saturated fat
41g carbohydrate
3g total sugars
3.5g fibre

Rhubarb Bread Pudding   Serves 4   (taken from *Food Facts for the Kitchen Front*)
(see page 74 for full recipe details)

And now...   a modern rhubarb pudding with home-made custard; rather than custard powder, you could serve this with biscotti biscuits to replace the bread.

Layered Rhubarb Fool   Serves 4

Put 4 sticks thickly sliced rhubarb in a saucepan with 2tbsp redcurrant jelly, 55g (2oz) diced dried figs, the grated zest and juice of 1 orange and 3tbsp water. Cover and bring to the boil; simmer over a low heat for 12–15 minutes or until the rhubarb is tender. Heat 300ml ($^1/_2$ pint) semi-skimmed milk in a saucepan until scalding, cool for 1 minute. Beat 3 egg yolks, 1tbsp clear honey and 1tsp cornflour together until creamy. Pour the milk over the egg, mix together and return to the saucepan; stir over a low–medium heat until the mixture thickens but do not allow it to boil. Add a splash of vanilla essence. Spoon the cool rhubarb mixture into the bottom of 4 individual glass dishes and pour the custard over the top and leave to cool. Sweeten 6tbsp natural yoghurt with honey and spoon on top of the cool custard. Sprinkle with 2tsp chopped almonds and chill until required.

NUTRITIONAL VALUE
245 cals
7g protein
10g fat

3g saturated fat
34g carbohydrate
32g total sugars
1.5g fibre

Sunday Lunch and Leftovers

A Sunday joint was a real treat. Cookery publications gave various suggestions for utilising every scrap of meat from the bone to avoid waste. In **Cooking in War-time,** Elizabeth Craig, a well known cookery writer during and after the war, suggested various ways to use up the remains of a joint: *'If you're ever able to have a joint on Sunday, don't always serve up the remains cold on the following day even though Monday's washing day. Do it up once in a while for a change.'*

* Slice and re-heat in a highly seasoned sauce. Serve with mashed potatoes

* Cut into inch squares and re-heat in curry sauce. Serve with boiled potatoes in their jackets or boiled rice

* Dice and re-heat in freshly-made white sauce, flavoured with onion. Add drained canned peas to taste. Serve in hot patty cases or on toast

And now...   We serve a re-heated dish as a rechauffé. Using up leftovers from the fridge requires just a little imagination. Food that has been cooked once before needs careful handling. The food isn't being re-cooked but only re-heated, so it must always be served piping hot. Flavour and lost moisture need to be replaced. Spices are a good option, as are sauces and leftover gravy.

Ham and Pickle Pie   Serves 4

Dice 225g (8oz) ham or gammon. Mix together with 3 finely sliced spring onions, 5tbsp spicy mango chutney and 1tbsp chopped parsley. Pile into a dish and top with 675g (1½lb) mashed King Edward potatoes, seasoned with 30g (1oz) grated mature cheddar cheese and 3tbsp natural yoghurt. Serve with a seasonal green vegetable or salad.

NUTRITIONAL VALUE
316 cals
19g protein
16g fat

8g saturated fat
26g carbohydrate
7g total sugars
1.5g fibre

Spring Salads

Salads became an important part of the diet as the nutritional value of leaves and other ingredients was essential.

SALAD SUGGESTIONS *(Ministry of Food, War Cookery Leaflet Number 5)*

Young dandelions make a delightful salad by themselves. Cut off the roots, wash the clusters of leaves well, dry in a cloth and toss in a quick dressing. For a more substantial salad, add fresh grated carrot, grated raw parsnip or grated raw swede, diced cooked potato and a few chopped spring onions.

And now...   Dandelion leaves – along with other bitter leaves – make fabulous, refreshing salads. In the spring the other leaf to look out for in woodland areas is wild garlic. In this adaptation you can make the most of any leaf, such as dandelions, young rocket and spinach and the tops of young beetroot.

Mixed Bitter Leaf and Seed Salad   Serves 4

Toss together a large handful of well washed and dried dandelion leaves and wild garlic (if available), rocket, baby leaf spinach and young beetroot leaves. Add 2 sticks of finely sliced celery and 1tbsp each toasted pumpkin and sesame seeds. Drizzle over 1tbsp lemon-infused oil and season with salt and pepper. Just before serving squeeze the juice of ½ a lemon on top and serve straightaway. Allow 1 handful of salad per person to serve as a light lunch or accompaniment to a main course.

NUTRITIONAL VALUE
70 cals
2g protein
7g fat

1g saturated fat
1g carbohydrate
0.7g total sugars
1g fibre

The Secret of Health and Beauty -Salads

SALADS ARE NATURE'S TONICS AND BEAUTY FOODS. They put a sparkle in the eyes, gloss on the hair and spring in the step. They're doubly important now ; they have not only to play their own good part, but take the place of fruit as well. A salad a day should be your rule ; a good big plateful, not just a finicky spoonful or so !

All green vegetables, and young, tender root vegetables, are at home in the salad bowl. Cabbage is not just a winter substitute for lettuce, it's much richer than that conventional plant in Vitamin C. Don't be afraid to experiment with salads. Test and taste — it's worth it.

Some salad health values

For Vitamin A : The richest are spinach, cauliflower leaves and parsley. Carrots, of course, but you absorb more A when they're cooked, strangely enough !

For Vitamin C : At least twice as good as oranges are cabbage, broccoli tops, parsley, kale, spinach, cauliflower (with the green), watercress, mustard and cress. As good as oranges : turnips, tomatoes, swedes. Good, but not so good as oranges : lettuce, parsnips, potatoes. Of course, that doesn't exhaust the list of good salad ingredients. All others are good, and give you necessary vitamins and minerals.

Prepare them this way

Tender leaves can be broken with the fingers, but avoid bruising or fine chopping or grating, as this destroys the Vitamin C. Root vegetables can be diced, sliced, or cut in slivers with a potato peeler No long soaking; the goodness seeps out. Wash as quickly as possible. Use as soon after buying or picking as possible, but if they must be kept, then wrap in a damp cloth and put into something airtight — a saucepan with the lid on will do.

Salad as a main dish

Salad as a main dish is refreshing, saves time, work and fuel. Include cold cooked potatoes and cheese grated or sliced, or cold diced meat, flaked fish, some sardines, pilchards or salmon, cooked dried beans. If some members of the family insist on "something hot" begin with some hot soup.

June Salad.
1 lettuce, 1 breakfastcupful finely shredded spring cabbage or spinach, 1 breakfastcupful cooked broad beans, 1 breakfastcupful diced cooked potato, a few radishes for garnish.
Line a salad bowl with lettuce leaves, and in it put the shredded cabbage or spinach. Arrange on this bed the beans and potatoes. Decorate with radishes and lettuce heart. Dress with mint sauce, or Victory mayonnaise. (See below.) *Serves 4.*

Salmon Salad.
Cut 3 cold cooked potatoes in cubes, dress with Victory mayonnaise (see below). Drain a ½-lb. tin of pink salmon, break in pieces, remove bones, mix with potatoes. Pile on a bed of lettuce or shredded cabbage. *Serves 3 to 4 people.*

Victory Mayonnaise.
4 level tablespoons dried milk, 1 level teaspoon salt, 1 teaspoon mustard, 2–3 shakes pepper, 2 tablespoons malt vinegar, 1 tablespoon water. This needs no cooking. You simply mix all the dry ingredients together, then add the mixture of vinegar and water and beat till you have a dressing of a smooth cream consistency. Use at once.

ISSUED BY THE MINISTRY OF FOOD (S64)

Mixed Vegetable Curry   Serves 4 (taken from *Cooking in War-time* by Elizabeth Craig)

Maggi was a popular brand of curry powder during the war. This is a good recipe not only for using up leftovers but also for creating a meat-free meal.

INGREDIENTS

2tsp (10g) curry powder

2oz (55g) dripping or cooking fat

1/2lb (225g) home-grown tomatoes, or beetroot

a bunch of spring onions (or 2–3 medium onions, if available)

1lb (450g) potatoes, sliced

A few sprigs of raw cauliflower (or a whole small cauliflower divided into sprigs)

Fresh shelled peas or bread beans in season, or a few small sprouts

METHOD

Melt the fat in the frying pan and stir in the curry powder, and fry a short while to draw the flavour. Next add the sliced tomatoes and potatoes and the remaining vegetables, stirring to absorb the fat and draw the juices. Add a pinch of salt. Cover and cook gently, with an occasional stir, until the vegetables are tender. There should be no need to add liquid with a fair proportion of watery vegetables, or root vegetables, in the varieties chosen.

Drain the vegetables and arrange on a hot dish, reduce the liquor and, if liked, season with sweet pickle or home-made chutney, as well as a good shaking of pepper. (Serve with a surround of well-cooked and drained rice or creamy mashed potato.)

NUTRITIONAL VALUE	
280 cals	7g saturated fat
9g protein	7g carbohydrate
14g fat	10g total sugars
	6g fibre

And now... the spring mint and spices in this updated recipe give it a zing.

Spicy Spring Vegetable Sauté   Serves 4

Soften 1 finely sliced onion in 1tbsp olive oil in a large frying pan. Add ¹/₂tsp each of ground cumin, ground ginger, ground coriander, turmeric, garam masala and 2 cloves crushed garlic. Cook for a further 2 minutes. Add 1 x 410g tin chopped tomatoes and 9 halved new potatoes, bring to the boil and simmer until the potatoes are cooked. Add 225g (8oz) shelled peas and a handful of young spinach, and season to taste with salt and pepper. Stir in a handful of torn mint leaves and serve with basmati rice.

NUTRITIONAL VALUE

163 cals

7g protein

4g fat

1g saturated fat

26g carbohydrate

5g total sugars

5g fibre

Offal

Many types of offal were appreciated during much of the twentieth century as they are highly nutritious. But concerns about vCJD are among the reasons for a steady decline in popularity and you rarely see recipes for offal dishes, apart from on restaurant menus.

In wartime lambs' and calves' kidneys, liver and sweetbreads were highly prized. Sweetbreads especially were regarded as a delicacy in some parts of the country. Offal was usually grilled or pan-fried in a little cooking fat or dripping – one recipe suggests using kidneys to flavour a risotto. A sweet wine such as Madeira and mustard are good companions for kidneys.

Kidneys with Mustard and Madeira Gravy   Serves 4
(see page 76 for full recipe details)

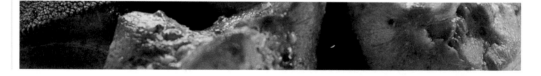

Poultry and Rabbit

During the war chicken was available but it was usually in the form of boiling fowls, mainly hens that were no longer useful as layers. Elizabeth Craig describes how to make the most of old fowls: 'Be sure that the giblets come with the bird. Make them into giblet soup, after browning them in a little hot margarine or bacon dripping, or else use them in the stuffing. The bird can be either cooked in a casserole or boiled and the carcass kept for stock.'

During the early part of the twentieth century chicken was regarded as a luxury and was usually served as the Sunday roast.

And now... During the latter part of the twentieth century chicken became an everyday food. With the skin removed it is lower in saturated fat than red meat. This recipe is devised from an idea by Elizabeth Craig. The original version suggests poaching an old fowl in spices then jazzing it up with vinegar and a selection of spices from the store cupboard. This version uses the same spices, but readily available chicken joints. Rabbit joints could also be used in place of the chicken.

Vinegar and Mustard Baked Chicken   Serves 4
(see page 78 for full recipe details)

Fresh Fish

In the 1940s fish consumption in the UK was considerably higher than it is now but was still light in oily fish. Today we have a wider variety of fish but tasto, rather than wartime limitations, has broadened our choice.

Casserole of Fresh Fish   Serves 4   (taken from *Cooking in War-time* by Elizabeth Craig)

INGREDIENTS

1lb (450g) cod, hake, gurnet,	5 large potatoes
haddock or ling fillets	1 medium onion
3tbsp margarine	3/4 pint (450ml) milk

METHOD

Wash and cut the fillets into suitable pieces. Peel and dice potatoes, and place in a saucepan. Bring to boil and cook tor 5 minutos. Drain. Melt fat in a stew-pan. Add the peeled and sliced onion and cook till slightly brown. Add potatoes and 1/2 cup (125ml) water. Cover and bring to the boil. Boil 5 minutes. Turn into a casserole and add fish, milk, and pepper and salt to taste. Cover and cook slowly in the oven until fish and potatoes are ready. Serve from the casserole.

NUTRITIONAL VALUE

450 cals	3g saturated fat
30g protein	51g carbohydrate
15g fat	9g total sugars
	4g fibre

And now... Fish consumption in the UK decreased dramatically during the twentieth century. Over-fishing has meant that some fish stocks are dangerously low although today's nutritionists encourage the consumption of fish in place of meat. Eating oily fish twice a week gives us a recommended intake of vital Omega-3. The wartime equivalent was to take cod-liver oil in liquid or capsule form.

Monkfish, Bacon and Sage Casserole   Serves 4

In an oven-proof casserole, fry 4 rashers of diced streaky bacon with 1 chopped red onion until soft. Add 4 small diced potatoes and continue to cook until the bacon is brown. Sprinkle with 1 tbsp flour and stir into the potato. Add 450ml ($^3/_4$ pint) vegetable stock, bring to the boil and simmer until the potatoes are cooked. Add 450g (1lb) diced monkfish or other white fish such as halibut or ling to the casserole, cover and cook for 5 minutes over a low heat. Stir in 3tbsp half-fat crème fraîche, 2tbsp chopped parsley and 1tbsp chopped sage. Adjust seasoning and serve with seasonal vegetables.

NUTRITIONAL VALUE
400 cals
37g protein
25g fat

10g saturated fat
7g carbohydrate
0.5g total sugars
0.5g fibre

Fish Pastes – Packed Lunches

Fish pastes, such as anchovy, shrimp or salmon, were popular standard fillings pre-war. In wartime their popularity increased as packed lunches became common.

Herring and Horseradish Paste   Serves 2 (taken from *Food Facts for the Kitchen Front*)

INGREDIENTS

2 cooked herrings

1tbsp milk

1tsp sugar

1oz (30g) grated horseradish

2tsp vinegar

A little salt

METHOD

Remove the skin and bones from the fish and flake the flesh carefully with a fork. Put in a basin, add the rest of the ingredients except the milk and mix thoroughly. Then add the milk gradually, stirring well with a wooden spoon. The mixture should be just thick enough to spread on the bread. Butter will not be needed for these sandwiches.

NUTRITIONAL VALUE
(assuming total weight of herring is 150g)
150 cals
14g protein
10g fat

3g saturated fat
2.5g carbohydrate
2.5g total sugars
0g fibre

And now...   With the twenty-first century's concerns about obesity and heart disease nutritionists advise that oily fish (high in Omega-3) such as herring, mackerel and sardine should be on the menu several times a week.

Sardine, Horseradish and Chive Pâté   Serves 2

Drain a 210g (7oz) tin sardines and put in a bowl. Mash with a fork. Add 1tbsp grated horseradish, juice of $^1/_2$ lemon, 1tbsp chopped gherkins and 1tbsp chopped chives. Season to taste with salt and freshly ground black pepper and serve with hot toast or on savoury scones.

NUTRITIONAL VALUE
173 cals
22g protein
9g fat

2.5g saturated fat
0.5g carbohydrate
0.3g total sugars
0g fibre

Vegetables

In late spring, broad beans were popular and well utilised, along with the last of the winter stocks including spring greens, cauliflower and other brassicas. The Ministry of Food gave advice on making the most of the nutritional value of vegetables:

As a pod vegetable, broad beans are valuable food. They contain vitamins A, C, and B1, and good vegetable protein. Freshly picked, when young, they are really delicious. Steamed, or boiled in a little salted water, they soon become tender, but be sure to leave on the outer skins of the seeds. Many people make the mistake of peeling away this covering skin, which deprives the dish of much flavour and food value.

Cooks were advised to boil the beans until tender and serve them with a piquant sauce made with cooking fat, a pint of stock made from the water in which the beans were cooked and a level tablespoon of flour.

And now... the skins of older podded broad beans are often removed as they are tough and bitter, but if picked young this is unnecessary. You can use olive oil in place of margarine.

Broad Beans with Minted Salsa Verde   Serves 4
(see page 80 for full recipe details)

Dried Fruits

Supplies of dried fruit were limited but most households had some in their larders and just a little did a lot to add variety to produce in season. The fruits would need anything up to 36 hours' soaking before cooking. The advice was to wash them in hot water, with the exception of dates, dessert figs and muscatel raisins, and then pour over just enough hot water to cover and soak for the time given on the packet, stirring occasionally. If sweetening was required, honey was recommended.

Apricot Compote   Serves 4   (taken from *Cooking in War-time* by Elizabeth Craig)
(see page 82 for full recipe details)

And now…   Use semi-dried fruits that don't require soaking. Fruit contains natural sugars, so only add sugar to taste if necessary. Choose any dried fruits as they lend themselves well to infused spices for a rounder flavour.

Fig, Apricot and Date Compote with Star Anise   Serves 4

Slice 110g (4oz) each semi-dried figs and apricots and halve and stone 8 dates. Put into a saucepan with 1 cinnamon stick, a whole star anise and the grated zest and juice of 1 orange. Pour over just enough apple juice to cover and bring to the boil, remove from the heat and leave to infuse for 30 minutes. Serve hot, warm or chilled with a dollop of fromage frais. Serve for breakfast or as a light dessert.

NUTRITIONAL VALUE
174 cals
3g protein
0.7g fat

0g saturated fat
42g carbohydrate
42g total sugars
4.5g fibre

Treat of the Week

Along with potato, home-grown oatmeal was a staple ingredient in the British diet. It was a solid, filling ingredient, inexpensive and easy to use as a replacement for flour in some recipes.

Porridge Scones   Makes 12   (taken from *Food Facts for the Kitchen Front*)

1/2lb (225g) cold porridge
1/2tsp salt.
1tsp bicarbonate of soda

1/4lb (110g) oatmeal
1/4lb (110g) flour
2tsp cream of tartar

Mix all the dry ingredients and work in the cold porridge. Roll out to a depth of about 1/2 inch, cut into rounds and cook on a hot griddle, or roll rather thicker, cut as before, and bake in a hot oven. Serve with jam.

NUTRITIONAL VALUE
75 cals
2g protein
1g fat

0.5g saturated fat
15g carbohydrate
0g total sugars
1g fibre

And now…   in place of filling traditional porridge scones, oatmeal added to the flour adds texture and flavour. The traditional method of shaping the scones into one round avoided wastage, but individually cut scones tend to be lighter and rise slightly better.

Oatmeal Scones

Sift 200g (7oz) plain flour into a large bowl with 1tsp bicarbonate of soda, 2tsp cream of tartar and a pinch of salt. Stir in 30g (1oz) oatmeal, 2tsp caster sugar and 30g (1oz) each dried cranberries and raisins. Make a well in the flour mixture and pour in 150ml ($\frac{1}{4}$ pint) semi-skimmed milk. Mix together with a knife until the dough is soft, but not sticky. Turn on to a floured board and roll to about 2.5cm (1in) thickness. Using a 5cm (2in) round cutter, cut into 12 rounds. Arrange scones on a floured baking sheet and dust with extra flour. Place above the centre in a preheated oven (220°C) for 10–12 minutes until well risen and golden brown. Serve with Carrot and Ginger Marmalade.

NUTRITIONAL VALUE
86 cals
2g protein
0.6g fat

0.2g saturated fat
19g carbohydrate
5g total sugars
5g fibre

Sugar Rationing

At various times during the war the sugar ration was increased so that home-made preserves could be made and stored for the following year. This was often organised on a communal basis and the resulting preserves were sold to raise money for good causes such as 'Salute the Soldier' and the 'Spitfire Fund', which were regular features of everyday life.

Preserves When Sugar is Short

To make with glucose: to each pound of fruit, allow $\frac{1}{2}$lb (225g) sugar and $\frac{1}{4}$lb (110g) glucose. To make with honey or syrup: allow $\frac{3}{4}$lb clear honey or golden syrup to each prepared pound of fruit. When fruit is soft, add the honey or syrup. To make with salt: allow $\frac{1}{2}$ tsp salt and $\frac{1}{4}$lb sugar to each pound of fruit. Note: if preserves made with honey, syrup or salt don't thicken to your satisfaction, add for every pound of fruit used $\frac{1}{2}$oz small tapioca, soaked overnight in cold water to cover, after adding salt and sugar.

And now... Traditional marmalade was in short supply during the war as Seville oranges were hard to get. Vegetables including parsnips and beetroot were used to make an alternative to the traditional preserve. This is a version with a ginger twist.

Carrot and Ginger Marmalade

Simmer 225g (8oz) grated carrot in 300ml ($\frac{1}{2}$ pint) apple juice, 150ml ($\frac{1}{2}$ pint) water, 1tsp white wine vinegar, grated zest of 1 orange and 1tbsp chopped stem ginger until the carrots are cooked. Once the carrots are soft reduce the cooking liquid by boiling gently until it has evaporated away. Stir in 1tbsp orange blossom honey and whizz briefly in a food processor to chop it well. Serve with Oatmeal Scones. *(Note: best stored in the fridge. This mixture will not keep for any length of time.)*

NUTRITIONAL VALUE
127cals
1g protein
1g fat

0.2g saturated fat
31g carbohydrate
30g total sugars
5g fibre

Rhubarb Bread Pudding

Ingredients

$^1/_2$ lb (225g) stale bread
jam for spreading
6 sticks of rhubarb
$^1/_4$ pint (150ml) water

Serves 4

2tsp custard powder
$^1/_2$ pint (300ml) milk and
water

Method

1 Cut the bread into neat thick slices. Spread each with jam.

2 Cut 6 sticks of rhubarb into 1-inch pieces and stew these in the water until almost tender.

3 Strain the fruit, retaining the liquid, and lay the pieces in the bottom of a pie-dish.

4 Cover the fruit with a layer of bread-and-jam slices. Add a layer of fruit, then another layer of bread.

5 Pour the rhubarb liquid, which should still be hot, over the bread and fruit and leave to soak for half an hour.

6 Mix the custard powder smoothly with a little milk and make it up to half a pint with hot milk and water.

7 Pour this uncooked custard mixture into the pie-dish and bake in a moderate oven for 20 minutes. Serve hot or cold.

NUTRITIONAL VALUE
210 cals
6g protein
3g fat

1g saturated fat
43g carbohydrate
12g total sugars
1g fibre

Kidneys with Mustard and Madeira Gravy

Ingredients

6 lambs' kidneys
15g (1/2oz) butter
1tbsp olive oil
3tbsp Madeira

Serves 4

2tbsp crème fraîche
2tsp Dijon mustard
2tsp wholegrain mustard
200ml (7floz) chicken stock

Method

1   Remove the fat and membranes from the kidneys and cut in half. Using scissors, snip away the central cortex.

2   Heat the butter and olive oil together in a frying pan and sauté the kidneys for 1–2 minutes on each side, until the blood begins to seep.

3   Lift into a sieve and keep the kidneys to one side. Add the Madeira and chicken stock to the pan, bring to the boil and add the crème fraîche, Dijon mustard and wholegrain mustard. Season with salt and pepper and replace the kidneys and heat through.

4   Serve with a jacket potato and seasonal vegetables.

NUTRITIONAL VALUE
(assuming lamb kidneys are 55g each)
155cals
10g protein

10g fat
3g saturated fat
3g carbohydrate
3g total sugars
0g fibre

Vinegar and Mustard Baked Chicken

Ingredients

4 chicken leg joints
1tbsp balsamic or red wine vinegar
1/2tsp paprika
1/2tsp ground ginger
1/2tsp English mustard

Serves 4

30g (1oz) melted butter
30g (1oz) grated Lancashire or Cheddar cheese
55g (2oz) fresh breadcrumbs
1tsp Dijon mustard

Method

1 Remove the skin from the chicken joints and trim away the knuckle joint.

2 Mix together the balsamic or red wine vinegar, paprika, ground ginger and English mustard, and seasoning.

3 Brush this mixture over the chicken joints and arrange in a roasting tin.

4 Mix together the butter, cheese, breadcrumbs and Dijon mustard and sprinkle over the chicken. Bake at 180°C for 25–30 minutes or until the juices run clear from the chicken.

5 Serve with mashed potato and a seasonal green vegetable.

NUTRITIONAL VALUE
400 cals
37g protein
25g fat

10g saturated fat
7g carbohydrate
0.5g total sugars
0.5g fibre

Broad Beans with Minted Salsa Verde

Ingredients

340g (12oz) young prepared beans
150ml (¹/4 pint) vegetable stock

Serves 4

1tbsp extra virgin olive oil
grated zest and juice of
1 lemon
1tbsp rinsed capers
3tbsp chopped mint

Method

1 Cook the beans in the vegetable stock until tender. Lift the beans from the liquid with a slotted spoon and set aside.

2 Reduce the cooking liquid to 4tbsp by boiling rapidly. Whisk together the olive oil and the juice and zest of the lemon into the reduced cooking liquid.

3 Add the capers and mint and adjust the seasoning.

4 Serve with bread and a salad as a first course or light lunch to accompany sliced air-dried ham and salami.

NUTRITIONAL VALUE
81 cals
6g protein
4g fat

0.5g saturated fat
7g carbohydrate
1g total sugars
5g fibre

Apricot Compote

Ingredients

½ lb (225g) dried apricots
2oz (55g) blanched almonds

Serves 4

2oz (55g) sugar

Method

1 Pick over and wash the apricots. Soak in cold water for 24 hours. Next morning, place in a saucepan with cold water.

2 Add almonds, split in two, simmer till tender.

3 Draw pan to the side of heat. Add sugar and leave till dissolved, stirring occasionally.

4 Serve when cold with cream or custard sauce.

NUTRITIONAL VALUE
227 cals
5g protein
8g fat

0.6g saturated fat
36g carbohydrate
36g total sugars
4g fibre

EDITH·A·BROWNE'S

25 *Ways of Serving* POTATOES

6^D NET.

FOODS FOR SUMMER

Yet another attempt to get the public eating more potatoes, this time from the cookery editor of Modern Woman magazine, published in 1941.
(Authors' Collection)

In the summer of 1941 the National Loaf was introduced which was made using only wheatmeal flour. In March marmalade and syrup were rationed to 8oz (225g) per month and the cheese ration was reduced to just 1oz (30g) per week. People bought their cheese ration monthly after grocers and customers complained about having to buy such small amounts week by week.

With summer comes an abundance of home-produced fruit and vegetables. It is a time for preserving to avoid any wastage, and to keep stocks through the winter. All the berry fruits are harvested – strawberries, raspberries, blackcurrants and redcurrants, along with glut of vegetables including tomatoes, courgettes, beans, peas, peppers, sweetcorn, lettuces – the list is lengthy.

Summer

With the hope of good weather and a general rise in temperature, both wartime and modern summer recipes are informal, lighter and refreshing – for example lettuce rolls, vegetable tagine and a modern twist on coleslaw. We have chosen recipes that make the most of the abundance of seasonal home-grown fruit and vegetables. Our modern recipes also exploit the wide variety of imported ingredients that have become part of our daily lives, including spicy sausages and olives.

wartime recipes	modern recipes
Toad-in-the-Hole	Spicy sausage, tomato and olive Toad-in-the-Hole
Fishcakes	Mixed berry trifle
Fruit soup	Mustard and tuna tomatoes
Mock raspberry jam	Potato, sausage and red slaw
	Summer vegetable tagine
	Cos lettuce rolls
	Haddock and chive fishcakes
	Crisp and crunchy summer salad with tarragon
	Crab and root vegetable gratin
	Potato and rosemary bread
	Raspberry and rosewater jam

EXAMPLES OF A TYPICAL WEEKLY MENU IN SUMMER

Sunday	Spicy Sausage, Tomato and Olive Toad-in-the-Hole Mixed Berry Trifle
Monday	Mustard and Tuna Tomatoes
Tuesday	Potato, Sausage and Red Slaw
Wednesday	Summer Vegetable and Lemon Tagine
Thursday	Cos Lettuce Rolls
Friday	Haddock and Chive Fishcakes Crisp and Crunchy Summer Salad with Tarragon
Saturday	Crab and Root Vegetable Gratin Strawberry and Mint Soup
Treat of the Week	Potato and Rosemary Bread with Raspberry and Rosewater Jam

UNRATIONED EXTRA. "Now, mind you, this dish is rather in the nature of an experiment."

Evening News

Shortages encouraged an inventive approach to meal planning.
(*Evening News*)

Stretching the Meat Ration

Toad-in-the-Hole was one of a selection of special wartime recipes as it was a good way to stretch the meat rations.

Toad-in-the-Hole
(see page 104 for full recipe details)

And now...   10oz (285g) is four sausages and we probably wouldn't think twice about eating most of that each in one sitting. Our recipe uses the same amount of sausage but we have used other vibrant Mediterranean flavours to create a similar dish.

Spicy Sausage, Tomato and Olive Toad-in-the-Hole   Serves 4

Sift 110g (4oz) plain flour into a bowl with a pinch of salt, ½tsp smoked paprika and ½tsp baking powder. Make a well in the centre and put 2 eggs in the middle with 2tsp tomato puree. Stir together and begin to blend in the flour. Add 300ml (½ pint) skimmed milk to form a smooth batter, chill until needed. Take 4 raw Chorizo sausages or something similar, twist each in the middle and cut to create cocktail-sized versions. Place in the base of a large oven-proof dish, bake for 5 minutes at 220°C then remove from the oven. While the dish is still hot sprinkle over 12 halved cherry tomatoes, along with 1tbsp chopped basil and 12 stoned Spanish olives, and season with lots of black pepper. Pour the batter over the sausage and tomato mixture, bake at 200°C for 30–35 minutes. Serve with a large mixed leaf salad and some crusty bread.

NUTRITIONAL VALUE
429cals
15g protein
27g fat

10g saturated fat
32g carbohydrate
6g total sugars
2g fibre

Ways to Stretch the Sugar Ration

A Sugar-Saving Hint (taken from *Food Facts for the Kitchen Front*)

When you are using acid fruits for stews or pieces, it is worthwhile remembering that you can reduce the sugar needed by as much as one-third by the use of bicarbonate of soda. With stewed fruit add the bicarbonate after cooking and stir it in slowly to avoid frothing. Raspberries, redcurrants, plums and rhubarb need half a level teaspoonful. Gooseberries and blackcurrants need a whole level teaspoonful.

And now... tart summer fruits are the most refreshing and bicarbonate of soda is known to affect some vitamin content – add just enough sugar to taste.

Mixed Berry Trifle Serves 4
(see page 106 for full recipe details)

Tomatoes are easy to grow but they fruit in abundance and then need to be picked and stored. There were lots of recipes for using them in casseroles, salads and preserving. We have adapted a recipe from Food Facts for the Kitchen Front that utilises tomatoes as a light lunch or supper dish.

Mustard and Tuna Tomatoes Serves 4
Break up 210g (7oz) drained tuna in sunflower oil with a fork, add 4tbsp fresh brown breadcrumbs, 1tbsp each chopped basil and parsley and 1tbsp olive oil. Spread a little Dijon mustard on to 8 tomato halves and sprinkle with the breadcrumb mix, top with 1tbsp grated Parmesan cheese. Bake at 200°C for 7–8 minutes. Serve with a mixed summer salad with a jacket potato.

NUTRITIONAL VALUE
235 cals
19g protein
10g fat

2g saturated fat
18g carbohydrate
6g total sugars
2.5g fibre

Vegetables and 'Digging for Victory'
'Dig for Victory' and its successor 'Dig On for Victory' were highly successful government wartime campaigns which encouraged people to grow their own vegetables. Publications encouraging civilians to deal with shortages gave advice on preparing and growing vegetables. On the radio Mr Middleton gave talks on gardening. Many people were taking this type of activity on for the first time, so results were variable. Vegetable accompaniments were whatever was seasonal and available from a local allotment.

▶

An advert encouraging women to grow their own vegetables. It neatly demonstrates the changes that the war had brought to the type of crops produced by farmers in this country.
(Authors' Collection)

DIG FOR VICTORY

For their sake-
GROW YOUR OWN VEGETABLES

PRINTED FOR H.M. STATIONERY OFFICE BY J. WEINER LTD. LONDON, W.C.1. 51-2853

A variation on the Dig for Victory theme.
(IWM PST 0200)

Food was grown everywhere, in gardens, window boxes, and on the shelter.
'We used to grow veg on top of the Anderson. Potatoes, because of the deep
roots, you'd put in the garden, but bits and pieces you put on the shelter.'
(Muriel Jones)
(IWM HU63827A)

Potato Salads   (taken from *Food Facts for the Kitchen Front*)

For use in salads, either new potatoes or waxy varieties are most suitable. The golden rule is 'Mix warm and eat cold'. Steam the potatoes in their skins, then peel and cut them into dice ready for the dressing. If you have a little mashed potato left from the previous day, try whipping it to a thick creamy consistency with a little mayonnaise dressing, and arranging it in the centre of a green salad. It makes the dressing go further.

And now...   dressing potatoes when they are still warm helps them absorb lots of flavour as they marinate in the dressing.

Potato, Sausage and Red Slaw   Serves 4–6
(see page 108 for full recipe details)

Vegetarian Diets

While there were fewer vegetarians than today, people in wartime Britain ate more vegetarian meals as meat was rationed.

And now...   summer vegetables lightly cooked together with a small amount of lemon makes a refreshing, light evening meal.

Summer Vegetable and Lemon Tagine   Serves 4
(see page 110 for full recipe details)

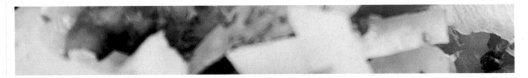

There were numerous recipes for stuffing vegetables such as marrows and parsnips. For the summer months cooked lettuce was also stuffed using a combination of margarine and oatmeal in a simple white sauce; it was then tied with string and baked in 'vegetable boilings' or stock until tender.

▶

Every spare inch of land had to be turned over to food production - including the domestic garden. (Authors' Collection)

Grow it Yourself

Daily Mail

Practical Instruction Book on

FOOD FROM THE GARDEN IN WAR-TIME

By PERCY IZZARD of 'The Daily Mail'

And now...   a quick and very light supper dish to make the best of the crisp and sweet cos or romaine lettuce.

Cos Lettuce Rolls   Serves 4
(see page 112 for full recipe details)

Fresh Fish

The challenge for the wartime cook was in getting to grips with cooking unfamiliar types of fish. Fish wasn't rationed but stocks were limited so some unusual varieties were offered; saithe, megrim and witch were alternatives to cod, while cod itself was sold as Icelandic Salt Cod or Salted Cod. Wartime varieties of meat such as corned beef and Spam are still popular today, but no one tried to sell the alternatives to traditional species of fish once normal service was resumed. Need we say more?

Fish was traditionally on the menu on Fridays. This is a long-established tradition, which has its origins in the Christian church. Consumption of meat was forbidden on Fridays, to mark the death of Christ on Good Friday.

Fishcakes   (taken from *Food Facts for the Kitchen Front*)

Take 1lb (450g) of boiled white fish. Cut into small pieces and mix with 5 cooked and grated potatoes, 1 egg, 2^1/$_2$oz (75g) breadcrumbs, 1tbsp white sauce, salt, pepper and chopped parsley, to form a stiff mixture. Shape into neat cutlets. Dip first in flour, then in milk, then in bread-crumbs. Fry in hot fat until golden brown.

NUTRITIONAL VALUE
(assuming 75g breadcrumbs)
450 cals
31g protein
15g fat

2g saturated fat
52g carbohydrate
2g total sugars
3g fibre

And now...   fishcakes have retained their popularity. Just about any combination of fish and herbs works well together.

Even the moat of the Tower of London was used in the drive to grow food. Here one of the yeomen from the tower is working on their allotment. There were even calls to dig up the Centre Court at Wimbledon, although these were rejected. (IWM HU63756)

Haddock and Chive Fishcakes   Serves 4
(see page 114 for full recipe details)

Summer Salads

Salad ingredients are at their peak during the summer. The official wartime advice was that salads gave health, vitality and (for women) made you more beautiful.

Crisp and Crunchy Summer Salad with Tarragon   Serves 4

Toss together 2 torn and washed baby gem lettuces, 12 radishes, 110g (4oz) halved cherry tomatoes, 1 finely sliced red pepper and 1 finely sliced red onion in a large bowl. Whisk together 2tbsp sunflower oil, 1tbsp runny honey, 1tbsp white wine vinegar and 1tbsp chopped tarragon. Drizzle the dressing over the salad just before serving. Serve with grilled meat or fish or as a first course.

Shellfish

Crabs, lobsters, prawns, whelks and winkles, among others, have always been a favourite British food, although today they are sometimes regarded as a luxury food. During the summer months of the Second World War shellfish would have been available to those living on or near the coast.

Elizabeth Craig gives a recipe using the traditional measure of 1 pint cooked crab (indicating the 'dressed' weight). This was mixed with a white sauce and surrounded by mashed potato to create Crab au Gratin.

And now... make use of different varieties of potato and other root vegetables.

Crab and Root Vegetable Gratin   Serves 4

Cook 1 peeled and diced Maris Piper potato and 1 large peeled and diced celeriac until soft. Drain and mash with a knob of butter and seasoning. Spoon into the base of 4 ramekin dishes and bake at 190°C for 10 minutes. Mix 225g (8oz) white crab meat with 2tbsp Greek yoghurt, a little fresh grated ginger and 1tbsp chopped chives, season to taste. Spoon the mixture on top of the potato and sprinkle with a handful of fresh breadcrumbs and 2tsp freshly grated Parmesan cheese. Return to the oven and bake for a further 10–12 minutes or until the crabmeat is piping hot. Serve with a side salad or fresh bread.

NUTRITIONAL VALUE

193 cals	4g saturated fat
14g protein	16g carbohydrate
8g fat	3.5g total sugars
	5g fibre

Summer Fruits

All summer fruits, be they berry or orchard fruits, would have been on the menu – making a light dessert using fruit was popular.

Fruit Soup   (taken from *Food Facts for the Kitchen Front*)

In summer-time a cold fruit soup is refreshing. It can be made from any ripe fruit, preferably of the berried variety.

Allow 1lb (450g) of fruit to every quart of soup required, and simmer until the fruit is soft. Then pass it through a sieve and either thicken with a little flour or cornflour, or simmer with 1oz (30g) of grain (such as sago or semolina) until it turns clear. Finely broken spaghetti or macaroni is also good as a garnish. Stir the soup until the cereal is cooked, then sweeten to taste.

A cinnamon stick or vanilla pod gives extra flavouring. For an apple soup use a little ginger. Chill the soup and serve as cold as possible.

NUTRITIONAL VALUE (For 1 quart)

81 cals	0g saturated fat
1g protein	20g carbohydrate
0g fat	10g total sugars
	0.5g fibre

Oranges – a real luxury. Any oranges for sale were usually reserved 'for children only' for at least a week. Parents could buy one pound for each child on production of the child's ration book. After that, if any were left, they were sold to the general public.
(IWM HU671)

And now... a refreshing soup making the most of strawberries, that do not require cooking.

Strawberry and Mint Soup   Serves 2–3
(see page 116 for full recipe details)

▲

◀ (previous page)

Tommy Handley counting coupons.
(*Radio Fun* Comic)

A Ministry of Food's Food Advice Service counter at Harrod's of Knightsbridge.
(IWM HU3809)

▶

A typical British Restaurant. In 1940, Communal Feeding Centres were set up to serve low-cost, healthy meals, which used non-rationed food. This proved a great success and early in 1941 they were rechristened 'British Restaurants'. By 1943 there were almost 2,000 of them, serving nearly 100 million meals a week. (IWM D12268)

Treat of the Week

The National Loaf was created in 1942 and was a wholesome bread made with wheat-meal although its heavy texture made it fairly unpopular. White bread was difficult to obtain towards the end of the war but there was always the option of making your own. To stretch flour to the maximum, cooked and sieved potato was often added to create a soft-textured loaf.

And now... potatoes and sweet potatoes combine well to make a soft dough with a hint of sweetness.

Potato and Rosemary Bread
(see page 118 for full recipe details)

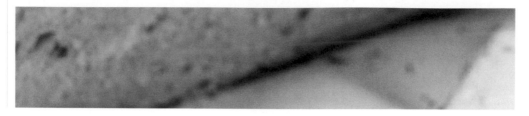

Jam Solutions

Fruit from mature quince trees became popular. To make the most of them, they were combined with tomatoes, another heavy cropping fruit, to imitate raspberry jam.

Mock Raspberry Jam   (taken from *Food Facts for the Kitchen Front*)

INGREDIENTS

2lb (900g) quinces

3lb (1.3kg) scalded, peeled tomatoes

5lb (2.3kg) sugar

METHOD

Chop the quinces. Slice the tomatoes. Place in a preserving pan. Add sugar. Stir over slow heat till sugar is dissolved. Boil till jam sets when tested on a cold plate.

NUTRITIONAL VALUE
(for the total quantity of jam)
9,329 cals
12g protein
5g fat

1.5g saturated fat
2,461g carbohydrate
2,461g total sugars
13.5g fibre

And now...   a traditional jam that would have been popular in wartime Britain with a little modern twist..

Raspberry and Rosewater Jam

Cook 2.7kg (6lb) raspberries in a preserving pan for 10–15 minutes or until the juices run and the fruit becomes pulpy. Add 1.8kg (4lb) warm preserving sugar, and heat until the sugar is dissolved. Bring to the boil and simmer for 12–15 minutes or until the jam reaches setting point. Remove from heat and add 4tbsp rosewater and leave to cool for 30 minutes before bottling. Pour into warm sterilised jars, cover and leave to cool. This will keep for 6 months if stored in a cool dark place.

NUTRITIONAL VALUE
(for the total quantity of jam)
7,767 cals
38g protein
8g fat

3g saturated fat
2,014g carbohydrate
2,014g total sugars
67g fibre

Toad-in-the-Hole

Ingredients

4 sausages
4oz (110g) flour
$^1/_2$ tsp salt
$^1/_2$ tsp baking powder
1tsp chopped parsley

$^1/_2$tsp crushed herbs
1 egg
1/2 pint (300ml) milk
1oz (30g) dripping

Serves 4

Method

1   Skin the sausages and reform each into two.

2   Sift the flour, salt and baking powder, into a bowl and stir in the parsley and crushed herbs. Make a hole in the centre and add the egg and half the milk. Stir together to form a smooth batter and once smooth, add the remaining milk.

3   Heat the dripping in shallow oven-proof dish until very hot. Add the sausages, pour over the batter and bake at 200°C for 30-35 minutes (till risen).

NUTRITIONAL VALUE
429 cals
15g protein
27g fat

10g saturated fat
32g carbohydrate
6g total sugars
2g fibre

Mixed Berry Trifle

Ingredients

Serves 4-5

225g (8oz) each black-
currants, blackberries and
raspberries.
1tbsp Port
juice and zest of 1 orange

2tbsp raspberry jam
300ml (¹/2 pint) low fat
fromage frais
honey to taste
6 ratafia biscuits

Method

1 Wash the blackcurrants, blackberries and raspberries and put into a saucepan with the Port, the orange and raspberry jam.

2 Bring the ingredients to the boil and simmer for 3–4 minutes.

3 Transfer to a large glass bowl or individual glasses and cool.

4 Sweeten the fromage frais with just enough honey to taste and spoon on top of the cooled fruit.

5 Crumble 6 ratafia biscuits and sprinkle on top of the fromage frais.

6 Serve well chilled.

NUTRITIONAL VALUE (TO SERVE 4)
245 cals
7g protein
8g fat

5g saturated fat
36g carbohydrate
29g total sugars
5.5g fibre

Potato, Sausage and Red Slaw

Ingredients

Serves 4

340g (12oz) salad potatoes
(Charlotte)
1tbsp olive oil
2tbsp red wine vinegar
2tbsp chopped rosemary
2 thinly sliced cooked cold
Cumberland sausages

55g (2oz) each sliced chorizo
and shreds of prosciutto
225g (8oz) finely shredded
red cabbage
1 finely sliced red onion
4tbsp natural yoghurt

Method

1 Cook the potatoes and cut in half.

2 Toss the potatoes with the olive oil, red wine vinegar and rosemary. Season with salt and pepper.

3 When the potatoes are completely cold add sausages, sliced chorizo and prosciutto.

4 Add the red cabbage and red onion and toss together. Season generously and dress with the yoghurt.

5 Serve as a main course salad or as part of a buffet.

NUTRITIONAL VALUE (TO SERVE 4)
186 cals
7g protein
8g fat

2.5g saturated fat
23g carbohydrate
6g total sugars
3g fibre

Summer Vegetable and Lemon Tagine

Ingredients

Serves 4

1L (1³/4 pints) vegetable stock
1tsp each ground cumin and ground cinnamon
pinch of saffron
3 slices of lemon

6 halved new potatoes
1 Florence fennel
8 asparagus tips
225g (8oz) runner beans
1 red pepper
2tbsp each of chopped coriander and parsley

Method

1 Put stock into a large casserole and add cumin, ground cinnamon, a pinch of saffron, lemon and season lightly with salt and pepper.

2 Add the new potatoes, bring to the boil and simmer for 8–10 minutes.

3 Finely slice the fennel, shred the runner beans and dice the pepper.

4 Add the fennel, asparagus tips, runner beans and red pepper. Bring back to the boil and simmer for a further 3–4 minutes.

5 Adjust the seasoning and add chopped coriander and parsley.

6 Serve hot or cold with a bowl of couscous.

NUTRITIONAL VALUE
95 cals
6g protein
1g fat

0.3g saturated fat
16g carbohydrate
4g total sugars
5g fibre

Cos Lettuce Rolls

Ingredients

Serves 4

2 large Cos (romaine)
lettuces
2 spring onions, sliced
1 cucumber, diced
2 sticks of celery, sliced

55g (2oz) cooked Puy lentils
or bulghar wheat
$1/2$ avocado, peeled and
diced
1 chilli, chopped
splash of lime juice

Method

1   Trim the lettuces and break into individual leaves, wash and pat dry. Arrange on a large platter.

2   Mix together the spring onions, cucumber, celery, lentils or bulghar wheat, avocado and chilli.

3   Dress with a splash of lime juice and season with salt and pepper.

4   Pile the vegetable filling in a bowl and let each guest fill and roll their own lettuce leaves.

5   Serve with a salad and a little olive oil to dip if required.

NUTRITIONAL VALUE
95 cals
2.5g protein
4g fat

1g saturated fat
12g carbohydrate
2g total sugars
2g fibre

Haddock and Chive Fishcakes

Ingredients

450g (1lb) poached and
flaked haddock
450g (1lb) potatoes
3tbsp finely chopped chives

Serves 4

1tbsp each of chopped
capers, parsley, spring
onion and gherkins
150ml (¹/4 pint) natural
yoghurt

Method

1 Remove any bones from the haddock and set aside. Peel, boil and mash the potatoes and allow to cool.

2 Mix the potato, fish and chives together and season well with salt and pepper.

3 Divide the mixture into 8 and shape into rounds about 4–5cm across. Roll in a little seasoned flour, brush with cool melted butter and cover with a layer of fresh breadcrumbs.

4 Bake at 180°C for 15–20 minutes or until golden brown.

5 Serve with the yoghurt mixed with the capers, parsley, spring onion and gherkins.

Note: if you prefer, fry the fishcakes in a little oil until golden brown and heat thoroughly.

NUTRITIONAL VALUE (BAKED)
415 cals
29g protein
16g fat

10g saturated fat
43g carbohydrate
6.5g total sugars
2g fibre

Strawberry and Mint Soup

Ingredients

Serves 2-3

640g (1¹/₂lbs) strawberries
2tbsp fresh mint, roughly
chopped

juice of 1 lime
150ml (¹/₄ pint) natural
yoghurt
icing sugar (optional)

Method

1   Put the washed and hulled strawberries, mint and lime juice into a food processor. Whizz together until smooth.

2   Sweeten if necessary with a little icing sugar and chill until required.

3   Serve each portion with a dollop of yoghurt and garnish the top with sprigs of mint, dusted with icing sugar.

Note: a combination of any summer berry fruit works equally well in this light dessert.

NUTRITIONAL VALUE
65 cals
1.5g protein
0g fat

0g saturated fat
15g carbohydrate
15g total sugars
1.5g fibre

Potato and Rosemary Bread

Ingredients

Serves 4

1 large potato
1 large sweet potato
450g (1lb) bread flour
1tsp salt
1tsp sugar

1x7g sachet dried yeast
1tbsp oil
1tbsp freshly chopped
rosemary
300ml (1/2 pint) warm water

Method

1 Bake the potato and sweet potato at 190°C for 1–1½ hours or until soft. Leave to cool before removing the skins and sieving the flesh.

2 Sift the flour, salt and sugar into a large bowl and sprinkle over the sachet of dried yeast. Stir well.

3 Add the sieved potato with the oil, freshly chopped rosemary and stir into the flour.

4 Gradually stir in the warm water adding just enough to make a light but not sticky dough (you may not need it all).

5 Turn on to a floured surface and knead well for 8–10 minutes until smooth and elastic.

6 Leave to rise in a large greased bowl covered with clingfilm until doubled in bulk. Knead again for a few minutes then shape into a bloomer loaf.

7 Cut 4–5 slashes across the top of the dough. Transfer to a floured baking sheet, cover with oiled clingfilm and prove for 15 minutes.

8 Bake at 210°C for 35–40 minutes or until well risen and golden brown. Whencooked, it will sound hollow if tapped on the underside.

9 Cool on a wire rack before slicing. Serve with Raspberry and Rosewater Jam (see page 102).

NUTRITIONAL VALUE (PER LOAF)
220 cals
53g protein
19g fat

3g saturated fat
484g carbohydrate
32g total sugars
26g fibre

Making the most of the MEAT

...re are two important ways of making the most of First of all, by cooking it properly and secondly ...ow to "stretch" the meat ration. Unless the ... roasting quality it is better to cook it ...ds described in this leaflet. Ordinary ... for the following cuts:—
...ribs, wing ribs and best chine.

MAKING THE FAT RATION GO FURTHER

Fat for Spreading
BUTTER EXTENDER No. 1.
8 oz. margarine or butter
1 level tablespoon flour
Put 6 oz. margarine into
spoon. Melt 2 oz. in
and add milk.
5-7 minutes.
well unt...
BUT...

9

Number 11

DRIED EGGS
The Ministry of Food package contains 12 eggs for 1/9d. or 1½d. each.
This dried egg is pure fresh egg with no additions, and nothing ...n moisture taken away. It is pure egg, spray dried. ...ry highly concentrated form of food. They ...y-building material. They also help us ...fection because of their high pro... ...are especially g...

FOODS FOR AUTUMN

DOCTOR CARROT the Children's best friend

Doctor Carrot pointed out the healthy side of that particular root, especially for seeing in the blackout, but he was replaced by Walt Disney's creation 'Clara Carrot'. He was just too old fashioned.
(IWM PST 8105)

In 1942 the Ministry of Food took more control over the nation's diet, emphasising the health benefits of the increasing proportion of vegetables and fruit in the average diet. Young children were given blackcurrant supplements and extra milk. Very little white bread was made from April. Lend-lease goods, supplied by the United States, meant that tinned meats became part of the staple diet, and 2d (1p) worth of the meat ration had to be taken in corned beef.

Autumn

As the nights draw in and the temperatures drop, particularly at night, our autumnal recipes combine a mixture of comfort foods such as rice pudding and kedgeree, but also utilise late summer ingredients like blackberries, aubergines and tomatoes. Not only have we chosen methods of cooking that create warming foods, but we also introduce the modern (and healthier) alternative to shallow frying, of stir-frying lamb with aubergines and olives.

wartime recipes

Irish stew made with venison
Kedgeree
Woolton pie
Baked beetroots
Malted brown bread

modern recipes

Venison hot-pot
Creamed rice with blackberry or elderberry sauce
Leek and smoked haddock kedgeree
Lord Woolton cobbler
Potato crust
Smoked fish and saffron pie
Hot beetroot with horseradish
Parsnip and sage
Lamb, aubergine and olive stir-fry

A TYPICAL WEEKLY MENU IN AUTUMN

Sunday	Venison Hot-pot Creamed Rice Pudding with Blackberry or Elderberry Sauce
Monday	Corned Beef and Chilli Rosti
Tuesday	Leek and Smoked Haddock Kedgeree
Wednesday	Lord Woolton Cobbler
Thursday	Potato Piglets
Friday	Smoked Fish and Saffron Pie Hot Beetroot with Horseradish
Saturday	Parsnip and Sage Soup Lamb, Aubergine and Olive Stir-fry

At the beginning of the Second World War venison was considered a luxury. It wouldn't have been in particularly abundant supply but it was home-grown and therefore available from estates with deer herds. It was also available from poachers, and there were many more of them than had been around in peacetime. Most game is lean and provides a good low fat alternative to other domestic red meats.

Irish Stew made with Venison   Serves 6–8

(taken from *Food Facts for the Kitchen Front*)

INGREDIENTS

2lb (900g) rib of venison

2lb (900g) mixed root vegetables

2lb (900g) potatoes

METHOD

Soak rib of venison in salt water for an hour. Cook meat slowly for about 2 hours in sufficient water to cover it. Put aside till cold and remove all the fat. Add the mixed root vegetables, prepared and sliced, and boil for $1/2$ hour. Add the raw scrubbed potatoes and simmer till potatoes are cooked.

NUTRITIONAL VALUE (900g of meat)

479 cals	2g saturated fat
56g protein	56g carbohydrate
6g fat	18g total sugars
	8g fibre

And now...   venison is usually available, trimmed and ready boned and often diced or in steaks. The flavour works well with herbs, particularly sage. Vension is farmed and therefore available during much of the year.

Venison Hot-pot   Serves 4–5

Thinly peel and slice 4 small King Edward potatoes and 2 small parsnips. Lightly butter a 1.7L (4 pint) oven-proof casserole. Layer the sliced potatoes and parsnips with 1 sliced onion, 15g ($1/2$oz) dried porcini mushrooms (optional), 1tbsp chopped sage and seasoning in the base of the casserole. Brown 450g (1lb) diced venison in 1tbsp sunflower oil, then place on the potato base and pour over 450ml ($3/4$ pint) each of cider and beef stock. Bake at 170°C for $11/2$–2 hours or until the potatoes are cooked and the venison tender. Add more stock if the hot-pot begins to dry out too much. Serve with braised red cabbage or another seasonal vegetable.

NUTRITIONAL VALUE

400 cals	3g saturated fat
32g protein	49g carbohydrate
8g fat	8g total sugars
	5g fibre

Milk Puddings and Seasonal Fruit

The nation was encouraged to make puddings from time to time. The official line was that they had a place in creating energy in the body but were not essential to maintain a balanced diet. Variety could be added with food growing in the hedgerows including elderberries, sloes, hips and haws, and blackberry picking became a favourite pastime.

Fruit farming was a major activity of the Women's Land Army, whose members took proficiency tests which included propagation, pests and diseases. 'Spraying is one of the nastiest jobs on the land. . . . Fruit-picking . . . must rank as one of the pleasantest,' said Vita Sackville-West in *'The Women's Land Army'* (Michael Joseph 1944). She went on:

The best moments of the fruit-picker's season arrives with the pears and apples . . . they must not be bruised, these Coxes, these Blenheims, these Ribstons, these Ellison's Orange, these Superbs, these Beauties of Bath; nor must the big cookers, Bramley's Seedling, Lord Derby, Newton Wonder, Peasgood Nonsuch, Beauty of Kent: an apple bruised is an apple lost.

Citrus fruits, which were imported, disappeared almost completely so home-grown fruit such as apples, pears, plums, cherries, blackberries, blackcurrants and rhubarb were a vital part of the wartime diet.

And now... Milk puddings have been a popular nursery food for many centuries – and you either love them or hate them. Comfort foods including sago, semolina and tapioca were popular during the war because they are filling. Blancmange and junket were also popular but rice pudding, then and now, is probably the most popular milk pudding of the lot.

Creamed Rice with Blackberry or Elderberry Sauce

Put 45g (1½oz) pudding rice into a heavy-based casserole. Add 600ml (1 pint) skimmed milk and a split vanilla pod. Cook very slowly over a low heat, stirring from time to time until the rice has absorbed the milk and is creamy in consistency. Remove the vanilla pod and stir in 1–2tbsp caster sugar. Put 225g (8oz) blackberries (or elderberries) into a saucepan with 2tbsp red fruit jam, and stir over a low heat until the fruit begins to soften. Rub through a sieve. Serve with the warm rice pudding.

NUTRITIONAL VALUE
155 cals
6g protein
1g fat

0.5g saturated fat
32g carbohydrate
22g total sugars
2g fibre

Your Children's
FOOD IN WARTIME

Some families had to be encouraged to take up the ministry's welfare scheme, which gave such things as orange juice to children.
(NA Image Library INF 13/143 (4))

'Milk of course, but don't forget Cod Liver Oil & Orange Juice'

WELFARE FOODS SERVICE
ISSUED BY THE MINISTRY OF FOOD

Printed for H.M. Stationery Office by Fosh & Cross Ltd., London. 51-2577.

Your Children's
FOOD IN WARTIME

You want your children to be healthy and happy, of course; and to grow up strong and sturdy. Do you know that **all** that depends very largely upon the food you give them now, and the food habits you help them to form? By following the few simple rules given in this leaflet, you can do much to make sure that your children build sound constitutions and healthy, active bodies.

Why is a child's food so vitally important?

1. Because a child develops bones, muscles and teeth entirely from food. Through the mother before birth, and in the diet of early and late childhood.

2. A child's food must also provide for the daily upkeep of the body, for protection against illness and for the supply of energy for almost ceaseless activity.

3. The younger the child, the smaller the quantity of food that can be taken at one meal; therefore each food served must be of good nutritional value.

Foods that build bones, muscle and teeth

1 MILK

A. Take full advantage of the Government's Milk Schemes. See that your child gets all the " priority " milk he or she is entitled to at home, and that school children get milk in school wherever possible.

B. See that each child in the family actually consumes his or her full allowance of milk, and that it is not given to any grown-up.

C. Use the National Household Skimmed Milk as an extra when it is obtainable.

D. Use milk in vegetable soups and stews, as well as in puddings, sauces and drinks.

Number

MINISTRY OF FOOD

WAR COOKERY LEAFLET 10

Canned Foods and Corned/Bully Beef

A store cupboard supply of canned goods was suggested for each household. Foods available in cans included fish, soups and fruits such as apricots, blackcurrants and plums. Meats included corned beef, stewed steak, bacon, tongue, ham and meat roll, along with many of the vegetables that are readily available in cans today, plus evaporated milk and canned puddings. Imported goods included canned cheese and butter.

(Information supplied by the Canned Foods Advisory Bureau, 243 Regent Street, London W1. ARP Home Storage of Food Suppliers)

And now... We tend to view canned foods as somehow inferior, as fresh food is often promoted as best. But the story hasn't changed and canned foods are both nutritional and convenient.

Kedgeree   Serves 2
(taken from *Cooking in War-time* by Elizabeth Craig)
(see page 136 for full recipe details)

And now...   a modern twist on a classic...

Leek and Smoked Haddock Kedgeree   Serves 4

Heat 1tbsp olive oil in a large casserole, add 1 thinly sliced leek and 1tsp garam marsala. Cook for 2–3 minutes. Add 170g (6oz) basmati rice and cook for a further 1 minute. Pour over 450ml (¾ pint) vegetable stock, cover and cook over a low heat until the rice is cooked and all the liquid has been absorbed. Stir in 225g (8oz) cooked and flaked smoked haddock and 2 quartered hard-boiled eggs. Season to taste and serve straightaway.

NUTRITIONAL VALUE	
80 cals	1g saturated fat
21g protein	35g carbohydrate
6g fat	1g total sugars
	1g fibre

Foods from the Mediterranean

Pizza in the UK in the 1940s was almost unheard of; 'Italian Food' meant some types of pasta, notably spaghetti and macaroni. It was usually simply cooked, but importantly some recipes suggest using the spaghetti cooking liquid or 'spaghetti stock' to make a sauce in which to serve the spaghetti itself. There were also recipes for risotto, but the Italian arborio and risotto rice would not have been available in the UK at this time.

And now... Many Italian classics including traditional pizza, dozens of types of pasta and many typical ingredients from all regions of Italy have become household favourites.

Chestnut mushrooms with pasta and marrow   Serves 4
(see page 138 for full recipe details)

Woolton Pie   Serves 4–5   (taken from *Food Facts for the Kitchen Front*)
(see page 140 for full recipe details)

And now... using the same potato crust, this version has the addition of garlic, fresh herbs and bulghur wheat.

Lord Woolton Cobbler   Serves 4

Take 1 small peeled and diced sweet potato, 1/2 a small head of peeled and diced celeriac, a thickly sliced leek and 1 clove crushed garlic. Put into a saucepan with 1tbsp each of chopped rosemary and parsley, sprinkle over 55g bulghur wheat and cover with stock. Simmer for 12–15 minutes or until the vegetables are cooked and most of the stock has evaporated away. Season to taste. Pile into a large pie-dish. Roll the potato dough on a lightly floured board, cut the dough into triangles and arrange over the top of the vegetables. Brush with a little milk and bake at 200°C for 15–20 minutes until bubbling. If necessary grill for 2–3 mins until golden. Serve with steamed seasonal green vegetables or a salad.

NUTRITIONAL VALUE
432 cals
10g protein
16g fat

6g saturated fat
67g carbohydrate
10g total sugars
9g fibre

Swanson's
EVER-FRESH
BRAND

8 OZS. NET

Dried Whole Eggs

ARRIVAL
SIX DOZEN

SWANSON

EASY

MINISTRY OF FOOD
LONDON, W.I.

NATIONAL DRIED
PARTLY SKIMMED
MILK

MODIFIED DRIED PARTLY SKIMMED MILK
(HALF CREAM)

SHOULD NOT BE USED FOR BABIES
EXCEPT

ORLOX PLAIN SUET PUDDING
■ is a mixture of Self-raising ■
Flour and Shredded Suet

Manufactured by ORLOX PUDDINGS, LTD., RETFORD, Notts

This is an

ORLOX PLAIN SUET PUDDING

in a Utility Jacket

MAXIMUM RETAIL
SELLING PRICE - 6d.

Potato Crust

Cook 225g (8oz) peeled King Edward potatoes in boiling salted water until tender. Sieve 110g (4oz) plain flour and ½tsp salt into a large bowl, add 55g (2oz) chilled, cubed butter. Using the tips of the fingers rub the fat into the flour until it forms fine breadcrumbs. Drain the potatoes, return to the pan and mash over a very low heat. Sieve the potatoes and add to the other ingredients with ¼tsp freshly grated nutmeg and 1tbsp chopped chives. Gently mix together with your hands until it comes together to form a ball. Use as required.

Fish

Fish was comparatively more expensive than meat in wartime. Smoked fish was familiar, but limited to locally caught products including Finnan haddock and kippers. These were a breakfast or suppertime treat and there are many recipes for jugged, grilled or 'boiled' fish. A fish pie was an excellent way of using up leftovers of fish or potato from a previous meal.

And now...   We have a wonderful selection of smoked fish, but the traditional species of cod and haddock are still the most popular. Undyed fish has gained in popularity in preference to the bright yellow dyed product. Saffron – one of the most expensive ingredients used in cooking – gives this simple pie a very subtle flavour and delicate colour. Hard-boiled eggs makes this recipe complete. The quantities given here are more substantial than they would have been during the war, when smaller portions were served..

Smoked Fish and Saffron Pie   Serves 4

Poach 500g (1lb 2oz) fillet of undyed smoked haddock in 450ml (¾ pint) skimmed milk flavoured with a slice of onion, a bay leaf, some parsley and a small pinch of saffron. Lift the fish from the milk, remove skin and bones and break into large flakes. Melt 30g (1oz) butter in a large saucepan, and blend in ½tsp English mustard and 1tbsp plain flour. Remove the pan from the heat and blend in the strained milk. Put the pan back on the heat, stirring continuously, until the sauce comes to the boil. Season with salt and pepper. Stir in the fish flakes, 2tbsp chopped parsley and 2 peeled and quartered hard-boiled eggs. Turn into a large dish and top with 640g (1½lb) well-seasoned mashed potatoes or root vegetables. Bake at 180°C for 25–35 minutes or until piping hot and golden. Serve with a seasonal vegetable or salad.

NUTRITIONAL VALUE	
373 cals	10g saturated fat
30g protein	28g carbohydrate
16g fat	2g total sugars
	2g fibre

Saving Fuel

Ways of helping save fuel included making sure that the oven, when heated, was always as full as was practical. Neighbours frequently took turns in cooking in shared ovens to conserve fuel. Local bakers would make their ovens available at specific times to people in the district.

Baked Beetroots (taken from *Food Facts for the Kitchen Front*)

When the oven is on, try baking the beetroots, without fat or water, as you would potatoes, or wrap them in a margarine paper and bake as before. They will take about 2 hours, if medium-sized.

To serve hot: cut quickly into quarters, and serve in a hot vegetable dish with a little melted fat and a sprinkling of chopped parsley. Or pour a little thick white sauce over them.

NUTRITIONAL VALUE
60 cals
2.5g protein
2g fat
1g saturated fat
8g carbohydrate
6g total sugars
1g fibre

" *My Commando son thought he'd help me on the allotment—but it's been too much for him !* "

And now... beetroot is often sold cooked or pickled. It does take a while to cook and served hot with horseradish and balsamic vingegar makes a lovely lunch accompaniment to fish.

Hot Beetroot with Horseradish   Serves 4

Put 4 medium-sized beetroot in a casserole, pour over 600ml (1 pint) water, cover with a lid and pot-roast in the oven at 180°C for 1^1/2–2 hours or until tender. Scrape away the peel and cut each into 8 wedges. Mix together 1tbsp extra virgin olive oil, 1tbsp balsamic vinegar and 2tsp grated horseradish, season with salt and pepper. Pour this mixture over the hot beetroot and toss to coat. Toss the dressed beetroot with 70g (2^1/2oz) rocket leaves and pile into a serving dish and serve straightaway.

NUTRITIONAL VALUE
50 cals
1g protein
3g fat

0.5g saturated fat
4g carbohydrate
4g total sugars
1g fibre

Soups and Stocks

A nourishing soup is a meal in itself. And a very comforting meal. Well prepared, it can be warmed up in a few minutes for any emergency.

You can take it in a vacuum flask to the Air Raid Shelter. You can leave it ready to be heated when you return after the All Clear.

Soup saves you time – and money – now.
(taken from *Food Facts for the Kitchen Front*)

And now... We can learn from the wartime recipes and should think again before tipping vegetable boiling water straight down the sink; it can be used for other purposes. Bread works brilliantly in place of flour as a thickener for this soup..

Parsnip and Sage Soup   Serves 4

Peel and slice 450g (1lb) parsnips. Put into a large saucepan with 1 chopped onion, 2tbsp chopped sage and 1L (1½ pints) vegetable water or stock. Bring to the boil and simmer for 15–20 minutes or until the parsnips and the onion are tender. Add 1 medium slice white bread, crumbled, and season generously. Transfer all the ingredients to a liquidiser and whizz together to form a puree. Add 2tbsp chopped parsley and serve with thick crusty bread.

NUTRITIONAL VALUE
122 cals
4g protein
1.5g fat

0.5g saturated fat
25g carbohydrate
8g total sugars
6g fibre

Mutton, Lamb and Rendering Fat

During the war mutton and the younger lamb was in steady supply. The most utilised cuts of meat were the scrag end and breast, as they were the least expensive. Both contain plenty of fat and are good for braising, stewing or pot-roasting. To make the meat stretch further it was either cooked with a selection of vegetables or minced and used as a stuffing. As fat was in short supply, all fat rendered from the meat during cooking was clarified and then used for frying.

And now... We can't buy mutton easily today but we do have British and New Zealand lamb. We tend to trim off excess fat. Instead of hanging it out for the birds, this could be rendered in the oven and a little used to roast potatoes to serve with a joint. We have chosen a lean cut of lamb – leg steaks – for this recipe, but have stretched the meat with the addition of aubergine.

Lamb, Aubergine and Olive Stir-fry   Serves 4
(see page 142 for full recipe details)

Tea Time

Tea bread, scones and cakes were still on the menu but butter in baking had been replaced by margarine and fresh milk by dried eggs as some prewar ingredients became costly and unavailable. Precious butter would have been reserved as much as possible to spread (very sparingly) on bread.

Malted Brown Bread (taken from *Cooking in War-time* by Elizabeth Craig)

INGREDIENTS

3^1/2lb (1.7kg) wholemeal flour

^{1}/2oz (15g) salt

water

^{1}/2oz (15g) yeast

1oz (30g) malt extract

METHOD

Place the meal in a clean pan. Make a hole in the centre. Dissolve the yeast and malt extract in 1^1/2 pints warm water. Turn into the hole, and stir in about one-third of the meal. Cover with a clean cloth, and set in a warm place for about 2 hours. At the end of that time, add the salt (rubbed to a fine powder under a rolling pin) and mix in the remainder of the meal. Turn out on to a board. Divide into convenient-sized loaves. Place in greased loaf tins. Cover and allow to rise for 1 hour. Bake in a moderate oven for 45–60 minutes.

NUTRITIONAL VALUE
(figures are for the whole quantity)
4,883 cals
200g protein
35g fat

5g saturated fat
1,107g carbohydrate
33g total sugars
141g fibre

No Wastage

To make the most of every last scrap of meat and vegetable, wartime cooks were advised to keep a stockpot on the go at all times. Into this went vegetable cooking liquid or 'boilings', as well as peelings, bones, gristle, scraps of meat and dried onion skins. This stock would have formed the basis of many meat dishes and soups.

Beans and pulses were not in plentiful supply as they are today, but haricot beans and barley were both good staple store-cupboard ingredients.

Quick Soup (taken from *Food Facts for the Kitchen Front*)

INGREDIENTS

1 pint (600ml) vegetable boilings or water

1 teacup (200ml) milk (optional)

about ^{1}/2lb (225g) mixed vegetables

1 tbsp cooked porridge

^{1}/2oz (15g) dripping

1–2 spring onions

METHOD

Prepare the vegetables, then grate the root vegetables and toss them for a few minutes in the hot dripping over a low heat, with the lid on the pan. Add the diced spring onions and heat for another minute – 5 minutes in all.

NUTRITIONAL VALUE
90 cals
2g protein
6g fat

3g saturated fat
7g carbohydrate

Corned Beef and Chilli Rosti

Ingredients

Serves 4

225g (8oz) corned beef
3 medium King Edward
potatoes

1 onion, finely sliced
3tbsp sweet chilli sauce
1tbsp olive oil

Method

1 Mash the corned beef and mix with peeled, par-boiled and grated potatoes.

2 Add the onions and sweet chilli sauce. Season to taste.

3 Heat the olive oil in a large frying pan, and add the corned beef mixture.

4 Flatten with the back of a spoon and bake at 180°C for 25–30 minutes or until crisp. Grill for 1–2 minutes to colour the top if necessary.

5 Serve with a mixed green salad.

NUTRITIONAL VALUE
200 cals
16g protein
13g fat

6g saturated fat
17g carbohydrate
4g total sugars
1g fibre

Kedgeree

Ingredients

2oz (55g) rice
6oz (170g) cooked fish
1½oz (45g) margarine

Serves 2

1 hard boiled egg
salt and pepper
1tsp chopped parsley

Method

1 Rinse the rice and cook in boiling salted water till tender. Drain in a colander. Hold under the tap to separate the grains, then drain again.

2 Remove any skin and bones from the fish, then flake the flesh. Add the margarine with the rice. Stir over a low heat till piping hot

3 Add the parsely and season to taste. Roughly chop the egg white and add.

4 Serve on a hot dish with chopped parsley and the egg yolk sprinkled on top.

NUTRITIONAL VALUE
395 cals
24g protein
24g fat

8g saturated fat
24g carbohydrate
0.2g total sugars
trace fibre

Chestnut Mushrooms with Pasta and Marrow

Ingredients

225g (8oz) fresh pasta shapes
2tbsp extra virgin olive oil
110g (4oz) chestnut mushrooms, halved
225g (8oz) marrow, peeled and diced

Serves 4

1tbsp fresh rosemary, chopped
1 clove garlic, crushed
1tbsp plain flour
1tbsp Parmesan cheese

Method

1 Cook the pasta in lightly salted boiling water for 1–2 minutes or until al *dente*; drain and put to one side. Reserve the cooking liquid.

2 Heat the olive oil in a saucepan, add the mushrooms, marrow, rosemary and garlic. Cook over a low heat for 1 minute.

3 Add the flour to the mushrooms and stir in 200ml (7½floz) of the cooking liquid. Bring to the boil and simmer for 2–3 minutes.

4 Season to taste with salt and plenty of black pepper. Toss the mushroom sauce into the cooked pasta. Pile into a large serving dish, sprinkle with Parmesan cheese and serve.

NUTRITIONAL VALUE
250 cals
9g protein
8g fat

1.5g saturated fat
34g carbohydrate
2g total sugars
1g fibre

Lord Woolton Pie

Ingredients

Serves 4-5

1lb (450g) seasonal
vegetables, diced
3–4 spring onions, sliced

1tsp vegetable extract
1tbsp oatmeal

Method

1 Place in a pan the diced vegetables, spring onions, vegetable extract and oatmeal.

2 Cook all together for 10 minutes with just enough water to cover. Stir occasionally to prevent the mixture from sticking.

3 Allow to cool. Put into a pie dish, sprinkle with chopped parsley and cover with a crust of potato (see page 130 for potato crust).

4 Bake in a moderate oven until the pastry is nicely browned. Serve hot with brown gravy.

NUTRITIONAL VALUE (SERVES 4)
317 cals
6.5g protein
13.5g fat

5g saturated fat
45g carbohydrate
6g total sugars
5g fibre

Lamb, Aubergine and Olive Stir-fry

Ingredients

Serves 4

2 x 140g (5oz) lamb leg
steaks
1/2tsp ground allspice
1 large aubergine
1 1/2tbsp extra virgin olive oil

1 x 410g tin tomatoes
150ml (1/4 pint) brown stock
kalamata olives, pitted
a pinch of sugar
roughly chopped coriander

Method

1   Cut the lamb leg steaks into 3cm pieces, put into a bowl and toss together with the ground allspice and plenty of ground black pepper. Cover and set aside.

2   Cut the aubergine into 3cm pieces. Sprinkle with a little salt and leave to stand for 10 minutes. Pat dry with absorbent paper.

3   Brown the lamb in half the olive oil in a large casserole or sauté pan, and lift out on to a plate. Add the remaining olive oil to the pan and fry the aubergine over a high heat until browned. Replace the lamb and pour over the tomatoes and stock. Bring to the boil and season lightly.

4   Simmer over a low heat for a few minutes until the aubergine and lamb are cooked. Add a handful of olives, season to taste and add a little sugar if necessary and stir in the coriander. Serve with basmati rice or seasonal vegetables.

Note: this recipes works equally well with diced pork and chicken.

NUTRITIONAL VALUE
172 cals
17g protein
10g fat

3g saturated fat
4g carbohydrate
4g total sugars
2g fibre

FOODS FOR WINTER

By early 1944 many foods were in short supply. Fresh eggs were rationed at this time to 4 per person per month. Over half the nation's diet was made up of home-grown produce such as potatoes, cereals, fruit and vegetables. Potato Pete and Clara Carrot, the former a Ministry of Food creation, the second from Disney, encouraged people to cook with those vegetables which were particularly plentiful.

Winter

Cold and frosty short days sum up a typical British winter and our recipes are all about comfort foods that are both filling and comforting. We have included some winter warmers: a chunky soup, potato recipes, hearty stews and old-fashioned puddings. By December the game season is well under way, hence the use of pheasant in one of the recipes. In postwar years, celebrating Christmas has become the focal point of winter, bringing light and cheer – a stark contrast to the war years when many of the trimmings we take for granted today were in very short supply.

wartime recipes

Oatmeal drink
Stewed chestnuts
Hard-time omelette
Mock plum pudding

modern recipes

Braised pheasant with apples and cider
Carrot, honey and oatmeal pudding
Chunky winter vegetable and chickpea soup
Chestnut one-pot
Date and hazelnut tea bread
Potato and salami tortilla
Winter crunch salad
Potato piglets
Trout herb parcels
Slow cooked beef in stout
Baked sweet potato and honey

A TYPICAL WEEKLY MENU IN WINTER

Sunday	Braised Pheasant with Apples and Cider
	Carrot, Honey and Oatmeal Pudding
Monday	Chunky Winter Vegetable and Chickpea Soup
Tuesday	Chestnut One-Pot
	Date and Hazelnut Tea Bread
Wednesday	Potato and Salami Tortilla
	Winter Crunch Salad
Thursday	Potato Piglets
Friday	Trout Herb Parcels
Saturday	Slow-cooked Beef in Stout
	Baked Sweet Potato and Honey
Christmas Treat	Mock Plum Pudding

Game Birds and Other Wild Foods

Game birds for food were not just restricted to pheasant, partridge, wild duck, grouse, woodcock and snipe during the war. Advice was given about many types of bird that could be trapped and eaten if necessity required – these included moorhen, plover, curlew, coot and sparrow. Squirrel pie was among the recipes for furred game.

A recipe from *Cooking in War-time* by Ambrose Heath details an old country recipe for lark or sparrow pie – for which you need five dozen birds, arranged with bacon and seasoning, and with a pastry lid. Comparison with the four-and-twenty blackbirds is irresistible! In coastal areas people trapped and ate cormorants and shags but they were not particularly pleasant to eat, as they tasted very fishy.

And now... Populations of all species of sparrow, especially the house and tree varieties, have declined very rapidly in the last 25 years. More traditional species of game birds are regaining popularity.

Braised Pheasant with Apples and Cider   Serves 2–3

Heat 1tbsp oil and 15g (^{1}/2oz) butter in a large casserole. Brown a prepared pheasant, first on the breast side and then the underside. Lift out on to a plate. Add 1 diced onion, 2 cored and diced Cox apples and 30g (1oz) raisins to the pan and toss over a medium heat until lightly browned. Replace the pheasant and pour over 150ml (^{1}/4 pint) dry cider and 300ml (^{1}/2 pint) chicken stock, season lightly and add a bayleaf and a sprig of rosemary. Cover and cook at 180°C for 50–60 minutes, or until the pheasant is cooked. Lift the pheasant on to a plate and reduce the cooking liquid to a syrupy consistency. Skim away excess fat if necessary, and remove the bayleaf and rosemary. Cut the pheasant into joints and spoon the chunky apple and raisin cooking liquid over the top. Sprinkle with chopped parsley. Serve with mashed potato, braised red cabbage and seasonal vegetables.

NUTRITIONAL VALUE
570-380 cals
44-29g protein
17-11g fat

11-7g saturated fat
27-18g carbohydrate
25-17g total sugars
2.5-2g fibre

Oatmeal

Oatmeal was a popular, filling ingredient used not only in porridge but in baking, stuffings, puddings and to thicken stews.

Food Facts for the Kitchen Front tells us: 'Scotland gives us oatmeal, the most valuable of all our cereals, more nourishing even than wheatmeal flour.'

Oatmeal Drink (cold)

INGREDIENTS

3 pints (1.3l) water , 2oz (55g) oatmeal,
^{1}/2oz (15g) sugar

METHOD

Boil the ingredients together. Do not strain. Shake well before drinking.

NUTRITIONAL VALUE
(figures are for the whole amount)
280 cals
7g protein
5g fat

1g saturated fat
56g carbohydrate
16g total sugars
4g fibre

And now... We have seen a decline in the use of oatmeal in cooking, but it does add extra texture and thickens, and porridge is still considered one of the best starts to the day as it is so filling. This sweet thick and warming pudding is somewhere between carrot halva and a honey porridge.

Carrot, Honey and Oatmeal Pudding   Serves 4

Put 340g (12oz) peeled and grated carrots, a pinch of ground ginger and 750ml (1¼ pints) skimmed milk into a frying pan. Cook for 8–10 minutes over a very low heat, stirring from time to time to prevent the carrots from sticking. Add 55g (2oz) oatmeal and continue to cook until the pudding is thick and creamy. Pile into a serving dish and drizzle with 1tbsp lavender or orange blossom honey and sprinkle with 1tbsp toasted almonds. Serve straightaway.

NUTRITIONAL VALUE
180 cals
9g protein
4g fat

0.5g saturated fat
28g carbohydrate
17g total sugars
3g fibre

And now... a winter warmer – thick main course soup with a variety of winter vegetables and chickpeas in place of barley or haricot beans. Bacon fat would often have been used in place of oil to brown vegetables, giving extra flavour and avoiding waste.

Chunky Winter Vegetable and Chickpea Soup   Serves 4

Heat a large casserole with 1tbsp oil, fry for 1 minute. Add 225g (8oz) each roughly diced butternut squash, peeled and diced celeriac, peeled and diced swede and 1 thickly sliced onion. Fry over a low heat for 3–4 minutes to allow the vegetables to soften and colour lightly. Add 1 clove crushed garlic and ½tsp chilli powder and pour over 1l (1½ pints) vegetable stock. Season lightly and bring to the boil. Simmer for 8–10 minutes, or until the vegetables are nearly cooked. Add 1 x 410g can drained chickpeas and a handful of shredded Savoy cabbage and continue to cook for a further 5 minutes. Adjust seasoning and serve with a sprinkling of grated cheese such as Wensleydale and thick slices of toast.

NUTRITIONAL VALUE
150 cals
7g protein
5g fat

1g saturated fat
21g carbohydrate
8g total sugars
6g fibre

Store-cupboard Ingredients

Various types of nut were used to make casseroles, stuffings, etc. Hazelnuts were enthusiastically harvested, as were chestnuts in the late autumn and early winter.

Stewed Chestnuts   Serves 4   (taken from *Cooking in War-time* by Elizabeth Craig)

INGREDIENTS

2 large peeled onions
1lb (450g) peeled potatoes
Salt and pepper to taste
Stock or water

2oz (55g) bacon fat
1/2lb (225g) chestnuts
Cornflour or flour

METHOD

Cut a gash on the thick sides of the chestnuts. Place in a saucepan. Cover with boiling water and boil for 5 minutes, then peel at once. Melt the bacon fat in a saucepan, stirring occasionally. Add the chestnuts. Cover with stock or water. Season to taste with salt and pepper. Cover and stew very slowly for 1 hour, then thicken with cornflour or flour mixed to a cream with stock or water. Stir till smooth and boiling. Turn into a hot dish. Arrange a border of fluffy mashed potatoes around the stew.

NUTRITIONAL VALUE
(assuming 15g cornflour)
300 cals
4g protein
12g fat

7g saturated fat
46g carbohydrate
8g total sugars
4g fibre

Chestnut One-pot   Serves 4

Brown 12 peeled shallots in an ovenproof casserole in 1tbsp oil. Add 110g (4oz) shredded shiitake or chestnut mushrooms, 1 clove crushed garlic, 170g (6oz) peeled chestnuts, 2 small diced potatoes. Toss over the heat until lightly browned. Sprinkle with 1tsp flour and pour over 300m (1/2 pint) vegetable stock. Bring to the boil and simmer for 25–30 minutes or until the potatoes and shallots are cooked. Season to taste and sprinkle with chopped parsley. Serve with a seasonal vegetable and warm bread to soak up the cooking juices.

NUTRITIONAL VALUE
145 cals
3g protein
4g fat

1g saturated fat
25g carbohydrate
6g total sugars
3g fibre

Date and hazelnut tea bread   Makes 12 slices
(see page 154 for full recipe details)

Dried Egg

Dried egg became a staple during the war and some people even preferred them to fresh. By the winter of 1944, with fresh eggs rationed to four a month, the dried egg supply was limited to one box (approximately 12 eggs) per person. Like milk this was distributed according to availability, usually about once a month. Recipes using dried egg were legion and they were often used to make omelettes. Necessity made duck and goose eggs more popular than before the war.

Hard-time Omelette   Serves 2   (taken from *Cooking in War-time* by Elizabeth Craig)

INGREDIENTS

1/4lb (110g) cooked potatoes	1oz (30g) lard
2 rashers fat bacon	1 dried egg
1 gill (150ml) milk	Pepper and salt to taste

METHOD

Remove rind from the bacon. Chop and cook bacon till the fat runs in the frying pan. Add thickly sliced potatoes and cook, turning frequently, till brown all over. Mix the egg with the milk. Season to taste with pepper and salt. Pour over the potatoes. Cook for 10 minutes, loosening the omelette from the side of the pan if it is inclined to burn. Slip on to a hot dish and serve at once.

NUTRITIONAL VALUE

340 cals	11g saturated fat
10g protein	13g carbohydrate
26g fat	4g total sugars
	0.6g fibre

And now...   A potato-based omelette is still popular but would more commonly be called a tortilla. The addition of an extra egg in this recipe helps bind the mixture and creates a quick and easy supper for two; the onion and salami add extra colour and flavour.

Potato and Salami Tortilla Serves 2

Fry 55g (2oz) diced salami in a small (approx 20cm wide) non-stick omelette pan until the fat runs, add 2 sliced red onions. Continue to cook for a further 7–10 minutes or until the onions are soft. Tip the mixture into a bowl and add 225g (8oz) cooked diced potato, 150ml (1/4 pint) skimmed milk, 1tbsp chopped mixed herbs and 2 beaten eggs. Season well with salt and pepper. Return the mixture to the omelette pan and cook over a very low heat for 8–10 minutes. Check the base every so often and if it shows signs of burning, finish cooking the omelette under a grill. Serve with a seasonal salad.

NUTRITIONAL VALUE

178 cals	3g saturated fat
9g protein	15g carbohydrate
9g fat	5g total sugars
	1g fibre

Winter Salads

The hard leaves of chicory and celery were available during the cold months of winter. This recipe is an updated version taken from the Ministry of Food's War Cookery Leaflet No. 5:

Winter Crunch Salad   Serves 4

Tear open 2 heads of chicory or Belgian endive and 1 head of radicchio. Add 2 finely sliced sticks of celery and 1 sliced red onion. Toss together with a dressing made from the juice and grated zest of 1 lemon, a splash of olive oil and a pinch of sugar and dried mustard powder.

NUTRITIONAL VALUE
42 cals
0.6g protein
3g fat

0.5g saturated fat
4g carbohydrate
2.5g total sugars
1g fibre

Cooking for Children

There was great concern as to how food rationing would affect growing children. Several Ministry of Food pamphlets were published giving advice on how to create a balanced diet for the whole family. Jacket potatoes were especially popular with children and there were many wartime recipes with names that reflected their appeal to the young. They included the 'Jack-in-the-box' – a baked potato with whole sprats stuffed into the centre for serving. 'Piccaninnies'(!) were baked jacket potatoes with a variety of stuffings, such as tinned meat, fish and inexpensive sausage meat.

And now...   Adapted directly from a recipe in *Food Facts for the Kitchen Front*, this makes a great mid-week supper for the whole family and particularly appeals to children.

Potato Piglets   Serves 4

Scrub 4 large baking potatoes and using an apple corer, remove a centre core of potato (the potato removed from the centres is useful for soup). Spread the inside of the potato with a little mustard or tomato ketchup. Insert 1 Lincolnshire Chipolata into each potato. Prepare 4 large squares of kitchen foil, and place 1/2 sliced onion in the centre of each. Sit a stuffed potato on top. Season the potatoes with salt and pepper and wrap each foil parcel securely. Bake for 1–1 1/4 hours at 200°C or until the potato is cooked. Served with shredded blanched Savoy cabbage or baked beans.

NUTRITIONAL VALUE
300 cals
8g protein
10g fat

4g saturated fat
47g carbohydrate
3g total sugars
4g fibre

Hay Box Cooking

As fuel was in short supply cooks were encouraged to be conscientious about cooking times. Popular for many, many years in rural areas, a hay box was simply a box with a hinged lid or an old packing-case stuffed with a thick layer of hay and newspapers, which was used to finish the cooking of stews, soups, porridge, etc. This method took a long time and it was essential that the food had a good start on the stove. Vegetable soups would be started on the stove for 45 minutes and finished in the hay box for 4 hours. As a rough guide, food was cooked for one-third of the recommended cooking time on the stove, followed by twice the whole cooking time in the hay box. It was especially useful for those out working during the day – they could start cooking the food in the morning and come home to a cooked meal.

And now... The use of a hay box today would be considered haphazard and probably dangerous; the modern alternative is a slow cooker.

Slow-cooked Beef in Stout   Serves 4

Cut 450g (1lb) stewing steak into large chunks and brown in 1tbsp oil. Remove from the casserole and add 2 carrots, peeled and cut, 1 parsnip, peeled and cut lengthwise, 10 peeled pickling onions and 110g (4oz) button mushrooms. Toss over a medium heat to colour, then sprinkle with 1tbsp flour. Add 300ml (1/2 pint) stout or Guinness and 450ml (3/4 pint) beef stock, a pinch of grated nutmeg and 1tbsp malt vinegar. Bring to the boil and transfer to a slow cooker. Cook for 4 hours set at auto (the slow cooker starts at a high temperature and automatically lowers it during cooking). When the meat is meltingly tender, lift on to a plate with the vegetables and place the cooking juices in a casserole. Simmer, skimming off excess fat, until reduced and syrupy. Season to taste and then return the meat and vegetables to the liquid. Serve with wedges of crusty baguette and mustard, or with jacket potatoes and seasonal green vegetables.

NUTRITIONAL VALUE

238 cals	2g saturated fat
28g protein	14g carbohydrate
5g fat	8g total sugars
	3g fibre

And now... the original version of the following recipe uses potato rather than sweet potato, but both versions are rich and warming

Baked Sweet Potato and Honey

Mix 285g (10oz) cooked and mashed sweet potato with 1/2tsp ground cinnamon and 11/2tbsp Acacia honey. Stir in 30g (1oz) sultanas and 55g (2oz) washed blueberries. Sprinkle the top with 30g (1oz) roughly chopped walnuts and 2tsp demerara sugar. Bake at 180°C for 20–25 minutes. Serve with fromage frais. Sweeten with honey if desired.

NUTRITIONAL VALUE
163 cals
2g protein
5g fat

0.5g saturated fat
28g carbohydrate
21g total sugars
2.5g fibre

Trout herb parcels   Serves 4
(see page 158 for full recipe details)

Christmas During the War

Christmas was one of the few festivals that remained during the war, although by 1941 wartime restrictions had an impact on traditional decorations, present giving and feasting.

By 1942 only one family in ten could get hold of a chicken or turkey but the Ministry of Food and housewives all over the country did their best to create something of a treat for the family.

This light Christmas pudding is just as good today as it was during the war. The dried fruits were minced to make them stretch further and the addition of carrot gives this pudding a good texture. Other root vegetables such as pumpkin or parsnip could be finely grated and used instead of the carrot.

Mock Plum Pudding   Serves 4–6   (taken from *Cooking in War-time* by Elizabeth Craig)

INGREDIENTS

6oz (170g) grated raw carrot
8oz (225g) shredded suet
1tsp ground ginger
6oz (170g) minced raisins
4oz (110g) cup sugar
1/2tsp grated nutmeg
1/2tsp baking powder

2oz (55g) breadcrumbs
1tsp salt
1tbsp chopped, mixed peel
3^{1}/2oz (100g) flour
1 tsp ground cinnamon
Cold water as required

METHOD

Sift the flour with the spices, salt and baking powder. Stir in carrot, crumbs, suet, raisins, sugar, peel and cold water to make a stiff batter. Steam for 4 hours.

NUTRITIONAL VALUE
889 cals
5g protein
50g fat

25g saturated fat
110g carbohydrate
80g sugars
2g fibre

Date and Hazelnut Tea Bread

Ingredients

Makes 12 Slices

340g (12oz) self raising flour
pinch of salt
$^1/_2$tsp mixed spice
55g (2oz) butter
110g (4oz) dates, stoned
55g (2oz) hazelnuts, browned

55g (2oz) soft light brown sugar
1 egg
250ml (7$^1/_2$floz) skimmed milk
2 tbsp sunflower oil

Method

1 Sift flour into a large bowl with a pinch of salt and mixed spice.

2 Rub in the butter until the mixture resembles fine breadcrumbs.

3 Chop and stir in the dates, hazelnuts and sugar.

4 Make a well in the centre of the mixture and the egg, milk and oil.

5 Stir the liquids into the dry ingredients to form a batter. Spoon the mixture into a 1.3kg (2lb) greased and lined loaf tin.

6 Bake in the centre of the oven at 180°C for 1–1½ hours or until risen and firm. Serve in thin slices with jam or honey.

NUTRITIONAL VALUE
215 cals
5g protein
10g fat

3g saturated fat
30g carbohydrate
9g total sugars
1.5g fibre

Trout Herb Parcels

Ingredients

Serves 4

4 small trout, gutted
sprigs of fresh sage,
rosemary and parsley,
chopped
4 bay leaves

zest and juice of 1 lemon
1tbsp each of spring
onions, capers and gherkins
150ml ($^1/4$ pt) natural
yoghurt

Method

1 Carefully trim the trout and rinse under cold water, being sure to remove any visible blood.

2 Cut 2–3 slashes on each side of the trout, straight through to the bone. Arrange each fish on a large disc of non-stick baking parchment.

3 Sprinkle with the herbs and a few extra sprigs for garnish and top with a splash of lemon juice and a bay leaf.

4 Wrap each fish in the baking parchment. Bake at 220°C for 12–15 minutes or until the fish is just cooked.

5 Meanwhile mix together the lemon zest, spring onion, capers, gherkins and yoghurt. Season to taste.

6 Serve each fish parcel with boiled or steamed potatoes and seasonal vegetables, handing the sauce separately.

NUTRITIONAL VALUE
200 cals
31g protein
6g fat

2g saturated fat
5g carbohydrate
4g total sugars
0g fibre

Imperial to Metric Conversion Chart

The conversion tables below are approximate. To avoid confusion when preparing a recipe, it is advisable to use either imperial or metric units of measurement throughout.

IMPERIAL	METRIC
¼oz	7-8g
½oz	15g
¾ oz	20g
1oz	30g
2oz	55g
3oz	85g
4oz	110g
5oz	140g
6oz	170g
7oz	200g
8oz	225g
9oz	255g
10oz	285g
11oz	310g
12oz	340g
13oz	370g
14oz	400g
15oz	425g
16oz	450g
1½ lb	675g
2lb	900g
3lb	1.35kg
4lb	1.8kg
5lb	2.3kg

LIQUID MEASURES

Imperial	ml
1tsp	5ml
¼ pint (1 gill)	150ml
⅓ pint 7½ fl oz	200ml
½ pint	300ml
1 pint	570ml

OVEN TEMPERATURES

°C	Gas mark
70	¼
80	¼
100	½
110	½
130	1
140	1
150–160	2
170	3
180	4
190	5
200	6
230	7
240	8
250	9

General Index

Recipe Index